THE CROSBY: GREATEST SHOW IN GOLF

THE CROSBY: GREATEST SHOW IN GOLF

by Dwayne Netland
With a Prologue by Bing Crosby

Doubleday & Company, Inc.
Garden City, New York
1975

Dedication

To my son Peter, who regards golf as a
tolerable interim between hockey seasons

PHOTO CREDITS
Photographs were supplied by many sources for this
book, and we would like to acknowledge and thank
the various firms and individuals involved: Del
Monte Properties, Bing Crosby Enterprises, the late
Julian (Spike) Graham, William C. Brooks, Anthony
A. Roberts, Rey Ruppel, United Press International,
San Jose Mercury News, Steven A. Gann, John
Newcomb, Al Satterwhite, Wilson Sportpix, John
Hemmer, Wide World, Canadian Press Wirephoto,
Atlanta Constitution, Lester Nehamkin, Edward
Slater. Other photos were obtained through the
courtesy of the United States Golf Association, Cliff
Dektar, Fred Corcoran, John Swanson, Ed Crowley
and Shell Oil.

Library of Congress Cataloging in Publication Data

Netland, Dwayne.
    The Crosby, greatest show in golf.

    1. Bing Crosby National Pro-Am—History.
2. Golf—Tournaments—History.   I. Title.
GV970.N48   796.352'7
ISBN 0-385-11158-4
Library of Congress Catalog Card Number 75–9220

CONTENTS

ACKNOWLEDGMENTS

I'd like to thank everyone by name who contributed to this book, but the list would read longer than Bing's movie credits. Special acknowledgments, however, go to those whose assistance behind the scenes was vital, even though some are not mentioned in the text. I'm thinking particularly of Lillian Murphy and Leo Lynn of Bing Crosby Enterprises; Ted Durein, recently retired executive editor of the Monterey Peninsula *Herald* who has been press chairman of the Crosby for nearly thirty years; Cliff Dektar of the Los Angeles public relations firm of McFadden, Strauss and Irwin; Henry Owen of the 3M Company; Bud Harvey of the PGA; Carol Rissel and the people at Del Monte Properties; and Todd Thomas of D'Arcy-MacManus and Masius, who conceived the idea of the book.

I'm equally grateful to the many professional and amateur golfers and show business personalities for their anecdotes and personal recollections. The fact they were so willing to take many hours out of their busy schedules for interviews is a testimonial in itself to Bing. Thanks must also be extended to my colleagues in the press and to my associates at *Golf Digest,* notably William H. Davis, president; Paul Menneg, associate publisher; Nick Seitz, editor; John Newcomb, art director; Charlene Cruson, who ably co-ordinated all the efforts; and Joan Urban, whose assistance in the preparation of the manuscript was critical.

And, of course, my warmest thanks to Bing, not only for his personally written Prologue, but for his close and gracious collaboration from the very start.

—Dwayne Netland

THE PROLOGUE

by Bing Crosby

In the early thirties, having abandoned the rigors of the vaudeville circuits for the more prestigious posture of a film personality, I joined a golf club called Lakeside. A very good course indeed, located out in North Hollywood.

The membership was composed almost entirely of fellas in the entertainment business—actors, writers, directors, producers, cameramen, technical people. Actually, though, the financing, the operation, and the maintenance were in the hands of members who were substantial Hollywood businessmen—lawyers, bankers.

The professional golf tour in those days played a few Pacific Coast tournaments —the Los Angeles Open, the San Francisco Match Play and one or two others. The pros were always in our part of the country in the winter months.

I was struck with the idea of putting together a pro-am competition where the Lakeside members, supplemented by some local low-handicap amateurs and other golf buffs could partner fifty or sixty invited professionals in a best ball event. Most of the pros would be on the tour, but the list also would include any of the home professionals in the area who wanted to participate. Truth to tell, there weren't many club professionals at that time who were available or would be likely competitors. Maybe ten or twelve.

At that time, I had a home and a small ranch down in San Diego County, near a nice golf course called Rancho Santa Fe, in the same region where I was involved in building and maintaining a race track known as Del Mar. A pretty little horse hippodrome by the sea. So the locale seemed ideal.

Our first event was held in 1937 at Rancho Santa Fe, and the weather that day seemed to set the pattern for what was to occur with annoying frequency in the years

that followed: a small deluge. But we played somehow, slipping and slithering and bashing about and, happily, the rain stopped in time that evening for the big barbecue down under the pepper trees at the ranch, with suitable potables, edibles and impromptu entertainment.

The field included plenty of fellas with talent—fellas who could sing, dance or tell a story—and I must say the first party was a pretty good little soiree, lasting far into the night and necessitating the aid of the highway patrol to guide some of the more bibulous participants to their pads in Del Mar, LaJolla, Oceanside and San Clemente. Thus was born what was to become known as "The Clambake."

Why it was called the "Clambake" I'll never know, because there wasn't a clam in evidence. It must have been because we were near the sea.

The golf tournament, I believe, was a success if for no other reason than the opportunity it afforded the amateurs to meet and play with some great golfers of the day, and for the professionals to establish a social relationship with some of the people who played and supported the game.

I think the gallery, though not vast, was entertained. They saw at first hand some luminaries of the entertainment field, some sports figures, columnists and other people of note, thrashing about—some of them with ineptitudes ruthlessly disclosed and others playing quite competently. But indisputably we all had a marvelous time, and I believe it might have been good for the game.

We played at Rancho Santa Fe until World War II broke out and most sporting events were put aside for sterner concerns. After the war, we began thinking about resuming the affair. Since I was then a member of the Cypress Point Club, and had disposed of my interests in San Diego County, the ideal place to locate the event was obvious—the Monterey Peninsula, one of the most spectacularly beautiful places in the world, with two golf links whose fame was truly international: Cypress Point and Pebble Beach.

Bing has played golf for over fifty years. He competed in the 1940 U. S. Amateur and the 1950 British Amateur, and played annually in the Crosby until 1957. Once a 2-handicapper, he's now an 8.

In the spring of 1946 I received a letter from Ted Durein, who was then the sports editor of the Monterey Peninsula *Herald*. It read, "There is a group of sports-minded persons on the Monterey Peninsula who would like to bring a big-time tournament here. We wondered if you would be open to a suggestion to hold it on one of our courses."

I turned the project over to my brother Larry and later that year we met with the Monterey people at the home of my sister in Watsonville, California. The original purse was to be $5,000, but the PGA had legislated a $10,000 minimum in the meantime, so we went ahead in January of 1947 with a $10,000 pay-off.

Del Monte Properties was agreeable to the arrangement and has been our host ever since, and we are eternally grateful because I count the locale as the single ingredient that contributes most to its success.

Robert Louis Stevenson is said to have described the Monterey Peninsula as "the most felicitous meeting of land and sea in creation," and when you stand in back of the 18th green at Pebble Beach and look down the fairway, with the waters of Carmel Bay on the one side, sparkling in the sunshine, and the other side shadowed with the majestic pine trees, you must concur.

The names themselves—"Spyglass Hill," "Cypress Point," "Pebble Beach"—what images of glamour, appeal and beauty they evoke. To be allowed to stage a golf tournament in such environs is like the Louvre granting choice gallery space to an aspiring artist so he can display his efforts.

Of course, these handsome places are on the sea, and the weather can be capricious. Maybe violent is a better word. The winds can rise to gale force, bringing pelting rain, sometimes hail and sleet and, on one lamentable occasion, six inches of snow.

The 15th at Cypress. Its next-door neighbor, the 16th, gets the publicity, but this sturdy little 113-yarder is a favorite with both players and galleries.

These are the times when these rugged courses relentlessly examine a player's competence and determination, when survival rather than attack seems the important issue.

But maybe that's part of the character of the area and the tournament that makes it unique. Nobody asks me who won the event—it's always, "How was the weather?"

I think also the galleryites enjoy draping themselves in every manner of rain gear, parkas, mukluks, hip boots, balbriggans, pea jackets, space suits, ski pants, Antarctic survival gear and woolen longjohns, and watching with fiendish relish while great players, actors, athletes and executives lurch through the rain, lashing out desperately against the elements with only occasional success.

On some stormy occasions, I've heard spectators say proudly, while wringing out their stocking caps, "I went the full 18 today." But for many tournaments—in fact, most of them—we've had beautiful weather. Players in short sleeves. Maybe just a slight breeze. Sometimes a bit of wind—just enough for the golf to become an exercise in control and to demand expert and careful management of the ball.

I like very much what Pat Ward-Thomas, the distinguished British golf writer, had to say about Pebble Beach: "This links has a rare alliance with nature which always come to its aid when it seems defenseless."

You know, our event is sometimes described as a "fun" tournament—a description which I rather dislike, because it sounds too frivolous, it seems to me. I can't deny, however, that a great deal of fun takes place.

Phil Harris always brought his own caddie—a middle-aged chap who is, like

Phil, "a bit fond of the drop." This time I think he tried to train like Phil trains, but I think he was overmatched a bit because when he arrived at the first tee to caddie for Phil, it was quite apparent he'd had an early morning bout with the flowing bowl. It was not noticeable to Phil, however, and in front of the large gallery and the foursome he was playing with, he teed up a ball, looked down the fairway and took a slash at it. There was a brief silence, and Phil turned to the caddie and said, "Where did it go?" The caddie looked at Phil with glazed eyes and mumbled, "Where did WHAT go?"

I followed Jack Lemmon for a few holes on the occasion of his first participation in the tournament. Now here's a man who has made thousands of personal appearances, made many films and television shows and done Broadway plays, and in front of the gallery at Pebble Beach, he was in a state of complete shock.

On one hole he teed up the ball preparatory to driving, stepped up and addressed the ball, waggled the club for what seemed an interminable time trying to pull the trigger, and all of a sudden a stray dog burst from the gallery in back of him and ran right between his legs, across the tee, and back into the gallery again.

Jack never moved a muscle, but hit the ball and strode on down the fairway. I saw him a bit later and said, "Jack, it's really remarkable—the composure you displayed

Bing talks tee shot with son Lindsay, a onetime Crosby participant. Asked by Bob Hope why he allowed his dad to drive home one night after the rigors of a late party, young Lindsay replied, "He was the best we had."

on that tee shot on 15. That dog ran right between your legs and you didn't let it disturb you at all. You hit the ball anyhow." He looked at me in shocked surprise and said, "Was that a real dog?"

We used to have some beautiful parties, of course, during the tournament in the evenings. Big functions. One of which was Francis Brown's annual "do."

He lived up on top of a hill—rather a tortuous winding road to ascend or descend. I was with Lindsay, my thirteen-year-old son, when Brownie invited me to the party and I said I didn't think I could make it, because Linny would be too young to come to the party, and I didn't want to leave him alone. Brownie said, "Well, bring him and he can sit out in the kitchen with the gardener and the help and have a good time. They'll give him a nice dinner and he can rest there and you can take him home when you leave."

So I did, but the night wore on beyond what had been my original intention, and the first thing I knew we were coming down the hill and it was 4 A.M. The back seat was full of revelers, and Linny was in the front seat with me. We made it all right.

The next day Linny was gallerying Bob Hope's foursome, and Bob came over and said, "How did you get home last night?"

Linny said, "We made it all right."

And Bob said, "Well, you didn't let your father drive in the condition he was in."

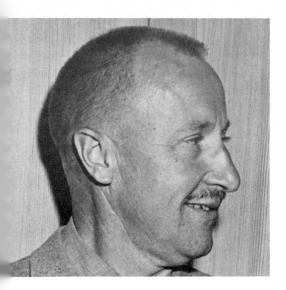

Linny thought a moment and then said, "He was the best we had."

On Sunday night after the tournament is concluded all the proceeds are taken to the Del Monte Properties office across the street from the Lodge to the accountant's desk, where the money is counted and stacked and put away. During the counting one year, a burglar broke in—a holdup man, I guess you'd call him—put a gun on the accountant and his assistant, bound them and started packing up the money.

The accountant feigned a heart attack and when the burglar reached down to loosen the gag on his mouth, the accountant kicked him in the groin and then fell upon him. With the aid of the assistant, they were able to subdue him and call the police to take the holdup man away.

The next morning, which was Monday, a bunch of us were sitting around the Cypress Point Club, talking about the tournament. Included in our number was an old chap named Stuart Haldorn. A very funny man. Didn't say much, but about once every month he'd come up with some wry, dry remark that would convulse everybody.

We got to talking about the tournament and somebody said it was a wonderful event. Somebody else said, "Yes, and the weather was superb," and somebody else said, "and a popular winner." Another said, "The golf courses were never in such fine condition." Somebody else said, "Thrilling shots" and someone else said, "Yes, I think there's no doubt. It's probably the best tournament we've ever had."

At which point Stuart said, "Well, I don't know. Seems to me that fella loused up the holdup."

I'm frequently asked, by journalists and others, what event, achievement or success

Ted Durein, press director of the Crosby ever since it moved to the Monterey Peninsula in 1947. It was Durein, a Monterey newsman, who made the original pitch to hold the Crosby at Pebble Beach.

Ringside seats at Cypress: spectators perched amid tangled trees to watch tee shots over the chasm on the 15th.

has been the most gratifying to me in my lifetime. Well, the answer is immediate. This golf tournament.

Here's the game I've played and loved for forty-five years, being played in the most beautiful environment imaginable on three world-famous links, by the best professionals, amateurs, sportsmen, and friends, and all for the substantial benefit of the most estimable charitable causes. When I think I've had a hand in all this, my cup runneth over.

And then I fill the cup up again and raise it in a grateful toast to the hundreds of Monterey Peninsula people who worked selflessly to make the tournament go. Without them, it would be simply impossible.

We have managed to raise over $3 million for various charities, including a foundation known as the Bing Crosby Youth Fund. At the beginning we built youth recreation centers and supplied funds for their maintenance. Later we aided every type of charitable institution. A few years ago we initiated an ambitious program that is particularly satisfying to me: the establishment of student-loan funds at nearly one hundred small colleges throughout the country. Most of the student recipients have repaid us after graduation, and many of them have contributed additional amounts to the fund.

This could not have been accomplished without the dedicated efforts of so many volunteer workers from the Monterey Peninsula area. Over six hundred men and women are necessary to our operation. I include among them our tournament committee—people who have donated countless hours of work without a nickel of reimbursement. The original committee consisted of Larry Crosby, Maurie Luxford, Dan Searle, Ted Durein, Gwenn Graham, Peter Hay, Pat Paterson and Scotty Chisholm. Later additions included John Logan, Joe Fratessa, Bud Giles, Chester Gillette, Roland Ingels, Dick Searle, Al Bergquist and Lee Darragh.

I'm also indebted to the corporate assistance of firms like Olympia beer, Oldsmobile and the 3M Company. Behind the leadership of president Ray Herzog, an annual participant in the tournament, 3M has been one of our major television sponsors for the past fourteen years and Olympia and Oldsmobile have been right behind.

Regarding our recent differences with the Tournament Players Division of the PGA, I never had any great hassle in our negotiations. Actually, I'm not a very good negotiator for our side because I've always been a fan of professional golf and its great players. I feel they are the major part of our cast. They should get all the money the traffic will allow and still leave a substantial sum for the charities our tournament serves. We sometimes go to the mat over how many pro-am teams should qualify for the final day's play. I've lost ground there, but I hope to rally. The pro-am feature of the tournament has always been part of its character and I don't like to see its importance diminished. Our format has been eminently successful and to change it seems unwise to me.

All of us feel that a book such as this, describing the history of the tournament and depicting its colorful and interesting aspects, is a truly wonderful thing to have. Without the support of *Golf Digest* and the tireless and talented efforts of Dwayne Netland, it would of course have been impossible.

Bing in a 1940 songfest with the Andrews Sisters and Irving Berlin. The Minnesota-born sisters were popular with radio fans in those days. Bing did a little work in front of the mike himself.

THE
STAGE

Morse's Monument

"In the Bible it says that God made the world in six days and rested on the seventh. There are some who insist that on the seventh day He created the Monterey Peninsula. There is no place on earth quite like it, no place that has three golf courses of such quality in so small an area. Your response to this angular chunk of land, shaped like the snout of a rhinoceros and jutting into the Pacific about 100 miles south of San Francisco, is instant and elemental. Even on a gray, overcast day it is compelling and seductive."

Those words are borrowed from Cal Brown's hauntingly literate description of the Monterey Peninsula courses in the January 1971 issue of *Golf Digest,* and they set the stage for a closer examination of the venues of Bing Crosby's National Pro-Am Tournament.

The Crosby sites are Pebble Beach, rugged and legendary, four times the site of U. S. Golf Association tournaments and scheduled in 1977 to hold the PGA Championship; Cypress Point, mysterious, a splendidly proportioned and artful mistress; and Spyglass Hill, a diabolical and controversial course which replaced the Monterey Peninsula Country Club as part of the Crosby milieu in 1967.

To those who come annually to watch the Crosby, and to the millions more who watch it on television, the scene is a stirring one. Hills and craggy bluffs tumble into the sea which ebbs and crashes against copper-brown rocks, casting huge white plumes and mist into the air above dozing seals and an occasional solitary beachcomber. Gray-boled and winter-green cypress trees cling to the soil in clumps or in stark individuality, bent and twisted by the

A rare bird's-eye view of Pebble Beach, with Carmel Bay, the coast line and the 18th hole in the foreground. Beyond are the Del Monte Lodge, the first hole and the forest.

wind and the spray. Here and there the headland splashes down into uneven, white-faced dunes. Yet surmounting everything is a sense of quiet, a curious intimation of settled spirit on the raging coast line.

The golf courses are part of the Del Monte Forest, 5,200 acres of private land developed by Del Monte Properties. The whole package was founded by Samuel Finley Brown Morse, a man of commensurate vision and dedication who had captained the Yale football team of 1906 and then heeded advice of Horace Greeley and headed West.

In 1914 Morse was given the job of liquidating the Monterey Peninsula holdings of the Pacific Improvement Co., which had purchased the property in 1879 for $35,000. Morse was so moved by the dazzling beauty of the land that he formed his own syndicate of San Francisco financiers, called it Del Monte Properties and acquired the forested peninsula and its seven miles of coastal shoreline.

From the outset, Morse insisted on high standards in use of the land. He hired a landscape engineer and personally planned a good deal of the two-hundred-mile network of roads and trails that cut through the area. And he established strict controls for the tastefulness and quality of all residences, controls which remain in effect today.

For over half a century Morse directed the affairs of Pebble Beach and its surrounding properties, his sometimes imperious ways earning him the title, "Duke of Del Monte."

Were it not for Morse, the Del Monte holdings might have been destroyed by short-sighted subdividers, or strung with carnival rides, shooting galleries, resorts and hot-dog stands. Under his firm hand, Del Monte Forest, though privately owned, was operated almost as a national park.

"Our most priceless asset is not so much the land," Morse once said, "but the beauty of the land." The Del Monte property is encircled by the famed seventeen-mile drive over which visitors may travel at $3.00 per car. No overnight camping is permitted, and no plant or animal may be "disturbed, injured, or removed." Deer roam freely through the forest and across the golf courses.

The grandnephew and namesake of the inventor of the telegraph, Morse died in 1969 at the age of 83, having left his imprint on the land for all time. His efforts for the construction in 1918 of the Pebble Beach Golf Links were described by the noted golf essayist, Herbert Warren Wind, in *The New Yorker* magazine:

In Morse's program to bring the resort's recreational facilities up to date, top priority was given to a new golf course—not just another new course, but a course that would make the peninsula no less synonymous with golf than Pinehurst. It is Morse who deserves the credit for allocating the choicest land,

Four Crosby VIPs of the post-war era: Jimmy Thomson, for years the tour's longest driver; Samuel F. B. Morse, the Duke of Del Monte; Jimmy Demaret, equally adept with a club or a quip; and Bob Hope.

the stretch called *Pebble Beach, to be used for the golf course instead of for posh ocean-front estates. His selection of architect was a young Californian named Jack Neville, a real estate salesman for Morse's company. Neville had no experience in building a golf course. Neville was picked because he was handy, and available. The way Morse figured it, a fellow who could play golf as well as Neville ought to be able to build a pretty fair golf course.*

The amateur architect created one of the world's premier golf courses, eight of its holes following closely along the twisting, cliff-edged shores of Carmel Bay. Combining the best qualities of British seaside links like North Berwick and Turnberry, it held the U. S. Amateur Championships of 1929, 1947 and 1961, and in 1972 became the first public links course ever to stage the U. S. Open.

At the time of the Open, Neville was still working as a salesman for Del Monte Properties. He took a few days off to watch the competition and briefly reviewed, in the San Francisco *Chronicle,* his early thoughts on Pebble Beach as a golf course:

"It was all there in plain sight. Very little clearing was necessary. The big thing, naturally, was to get in as many holes as possible along the bay. It took a little imagination, but not much. Years before it was built, I could see this place as a golf links. Nature had intended it be nothing else. All we did was cut away a few trees, install a few sprinklers and sow a little seed."

Pebble Beach Golf Links was opened in 1919 at a cost of $75,000, one of the great bargains of all time.

Just as Morse had planned Pebble Beach as a resort course, he had long envisioned the creation of a private golf club on his property, to be operated outside the province of Del Monte Properties. This brought about the founding of the Cypress Point Club, built in 1928 by a group of California financiers who had purchased the land from Morse and designed by the eminent Dr. Alister MacKenzie.

Morse was also instrumental in the birth of Spyglass Hill, the third and newest of the Crosby sites. Del Monte provided the bulk of the financing in conjunction with the Northern California Golf Association and hired Robert Trent Jones to design the course, which opened in 1966.

Spyglass Hill: New Kid on the Block

Much of the Spyglass Hill motif is taken from the literary work of Robert Louis Stevenson. Stevenson lived for a short time in the Del Monte Forest, gaining inspiration for his *Treasure Island* and other stories of piracy and derring-do. Standing on the highest ground of Spyglass, near Indian Village, he could see all the way across the bay to Santa Cruz. Stevenson's legend is perpetuated today, not only in the names of Spyglass holes such as Treasure Island, Billy Bones, Capt. Smollett, Admiral Benbow, Long John Silver and Jim Hawkins, but also in the Robert Louis Stevenson boys' prep school bordering the course.

The catalyst for the creation of Spyglass Hill was the Northern California Golf Association, which was seeking a permanent headquarters and site for its tournaments. Its members put up $2,500 apiece to assist in the construction costs of over $500,000 for the golf course and clubhouse. The NCGA leases the course for thirty days a year from Del Monte Properties to conduct its events.

Samuel F. B. Morse and Bob Hanna, executive secretary of the NCGA, conceived the name Spyglass, Hanna naming the holes after Stevenson's fictional characters.

Like Pebble Beach, Spyglass is a public fee course. Members of the NCGA and guests at Del Monte Lodge pay $10 green fees. The regular greens fee is $15. Over 25,000 rounds are played annually.

Robert Trent Jones visualized Spyglass as the crowning achievement of his

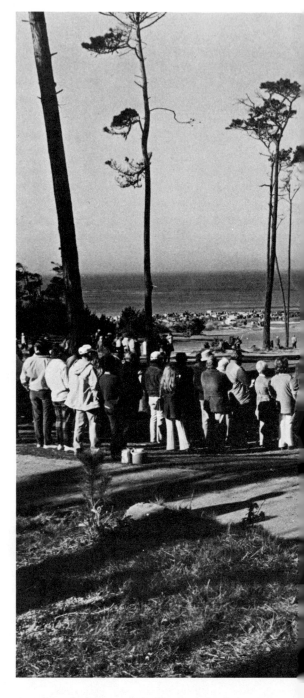

Action on the 6th green at Spyglass, the Robert Trent Jones course with the Long John Silver personality. In the background: the Pacific.

Elemental golf at Spyglass. The 4th green is set among the sand dunes, exposed to the capricious weather lashing in off the water.

distinguished and prolific career in golf architecture, a course in which the sea, the forest and the dunes all were brought into play.

Spyglass was under construction for two years before it opened on March 11, 1966, and Jones had problems. Fifty acres of Monterey pine had to be cut down and burned, a Del Monte road closed off, and some equestrian and jumping trails which ran through the forest abandoned. Jones surmounted the challenges.

The man who initiated the move to get Spyglass on the Crosby rota was Crosby himself, convinced that its earthy beauty and severity would complement the more refined aesthetics of Cypress Point and Pebble Beach. The course's difficulty became instant legend.

On a January day in 1967, the first year Spyglass was used for the Crosby, Bing approached Jack Nicklaus and said, "I'll bet you five you can't shoot par from the back tees in your first round at Spyglass."

Nicklaus accepted the challenge, inquiring whether Bing meant $5.00 or $5,000. "Either," Crosby replied. "The loser antes up to charity." Playing winter rules in his practice round, Nicklaus shot 70, 2 under par. In the tournament, which he won, Jack could manage no better than a 74.

The bet was compromised, as Bing remembers it, at $500, and he paid up.

"Spyglass will be one of the finest in the world," Crosby said. "It's got everything that a great golf course requires. It's two shots harder right now than Pebble Beach."

Crosby's assessment may have been a bit premature—it is pretty well agreed now that Spyglass was not ready for tournament play in January 1967. A drainage problem had not been resolved and the fairways were soft and heavy. The greens were immature.

Actor Jim Garner, who played to a solid 3-handicap for many years, observed another, more permanent shortcoming. "I feel like I'm walking uphill all the way around after the first hole," he said. Others complained of the long hikes from some greens to the next tees. "The second tee is a driver, spoon, and wedge from the first tee," cracked Doug Ford one day. "In New York I'd call a cab to go that far."

There was, all the same, a redeeming character to the course. The first five holes, constructed over sandy dunes along the

Pacific, were reminiscent of Pine Valley. Jones admits he sought to capture the feeling of Pine Valley in that sandy beach area. "To ignore such an opportunity," he explains, "would have been foolhardy."

The next thirteen holes weave through majestic pines, with water hazards created on the 12th, 14th and 15th. The 12th hole, a classic 180-yarder, was patterned after the Redan hole of North Berwick in Britain. The 13th is a muscular, 440-yard par-4; the 14th a long, double-dogleg par-5; and the 16th, perhaps the best hole on the course, a slender, 465-yard par-4 to an elevated green.

From the championship tees, Spyglass plays at 6,810 yards with a rating of 76.1 and from the regular tees, 6,377 yards with a rating of 74.1 The course record is 66, shot by Ken Towns and Dan Sikes in the 1972 Crosby and by Larry Ziegler in the 1975 tournament.

"Those were all great scores on this golf course," says Frank Thacker, the Spyglass pro since the day it opened. "People who play Spyglass can't believe how tough it is."

Thacker's favorite story is the one about the two doctors who teed off armed with three dozen golf balls. After playing six holes, they had to send a caddie in for a new supply.

Singer Andy Williams, who carries a 14-handicap, brought out a common complaint among the amateurs. "I can't reach those long par-4 holes," he said. "I have to play the 6th, 9th, 13th and 16th as par-5s. It's obvious this golf course was built for a much stronger player than I am."

Jim Murray of the Los Angeles *Times* phrased it pungently the first year Spyglass was used for the Crosby:

If it were human, Spyglass would have a knife in its teeth, a patch on its eye, a ring in its ear, tobacco in its beard, and a

blunderbuss in its hands. It's a privateer plundering the golfing main, an amphibious creature, half ocean, half forest. You play through from seals to squirrels, sand dunes to pine cones, pounding surf to mast-high firs. It's a 300-acre unplayable lie.

As the years go by, however, Crosby's original observation about Spyglass is coming true. The greens have matured and the course has developed its own personality. The problem is that Spyglass is like a shady woman. Once branded, she can't shake her reputation.

The pros, so critical of Spyglass in its early years, are beginning to appreciate the course. Bob Goalby, a veteran of many years in the Crosby, was ambling happily along the 16th fairway during the 1975 tournament, gazing at the scene around him.

"I hardly recognize the place," he said. "All the other times I've played here I was just trying to survive in the mud, to get around and get out. Today the sun is shining, the fairways are dry and the golf course is beautiful."

Cypress Point: Golf's Sistine Chapel

Frank (Sandy) Tatum, a prominent San Francisco attorney, vice-president of the U. S. Golf Association, chairman of the USGA Championship Committee and member of Cypress Point, was standing near the 12th tee at Cypress. He gazed at the sand dunes, the rolling woodlands and, just beyond, the crashing waters of the Pacific.

"Cypress Point," mused Tatum in a moment of revery, "is the Sistine Chapel of golf."

Few golfers who have played it would debate the claim.

The course is beautifully framed by the Del Monte Forest on its southern and eastern borders, proceeds westerly through the rolling sand dunes toward the ocean to the 15th tee. The 15th, 16th and 17th holes are played over inlets of the Pacific, and the 18th dissolves gently through scattered trees to a flagstick silhouetted against the sky next to the Spanish-style clubhouse that seems to have grown there among the cypress trees.

Much of the Cypress Point tradition has emanated from the 16th, a par-3 of 222 yards over the water to a large green at the tip of the point. The courageous golfer can elect to go for the green with anything from a driver to a long iron, but there is an option of a mid-iron shot to a plateau about 70 yards left of the green.

Surrounding that lay-up area, however, are treacherous beds of ice plant, a wiry growth of California shrubbery from which it is almost impossible to extract the ball.

The muscular Mike Souchak once lost a $20 bet with Julius Boros that he could dig the ball out of the ice plant onto the 16th green in one shot. "It was a cinch," Boros later told Bing. "It was Mike's first year in the tournament. He had never seen the stuff before. I had just come in off a practice round where I'd taken three shots trying to get the ball out."

Cypress was begun in 1926 by Roger Lapham, a president of the California Golf Association, and Marion Hollins, the USGA Women's Amateur champion of 1921. They founded the group which bought the property from Del Monte Properties and commissioned Dr. Alister MacKenzie, the Scottish architect, to design the course. Dr. MacKenzie completed his masterpiece in 1928 and three years later began construction of Augusta National under the supervision of Bob Jones and Clifford Roberts.

Located just down the 17-mile drive from Pebble Beach, at the western tip of the peninsula, Cypress is a private club, in every sense of the word. The course and the clubhouse are open only to the 175 members and their guests. The membership is a select clientele of established wealth, and the dominant theme is exclusive tradition. The initiation fee for new members is $10,000, although the monthly dues are a relatively modest $70. Golf is the only game available. There are no swimming pools, tennis courts or other diversions.

The shortest of the three Crosby courses, Cypress measures only 6,462 yards from the back tees and 6,265 from the member tees, with a par and rating of 72. The competitive course record is 65 shot by Bill Nary during the 1949 Crosby, although Ben Hogan and Bob Lunn have recorded 63s in practice rounds.

Lunn was accompanied by his friend and tutor, Sacramento pro Tom LoPresti, who became so enthused over his partner's performance that he began taking a swig of Scotch each time Lunn birdied a hole. As Lunn walked onto the 16th tee, LoPresti took another deep swallow. "What's that for?"

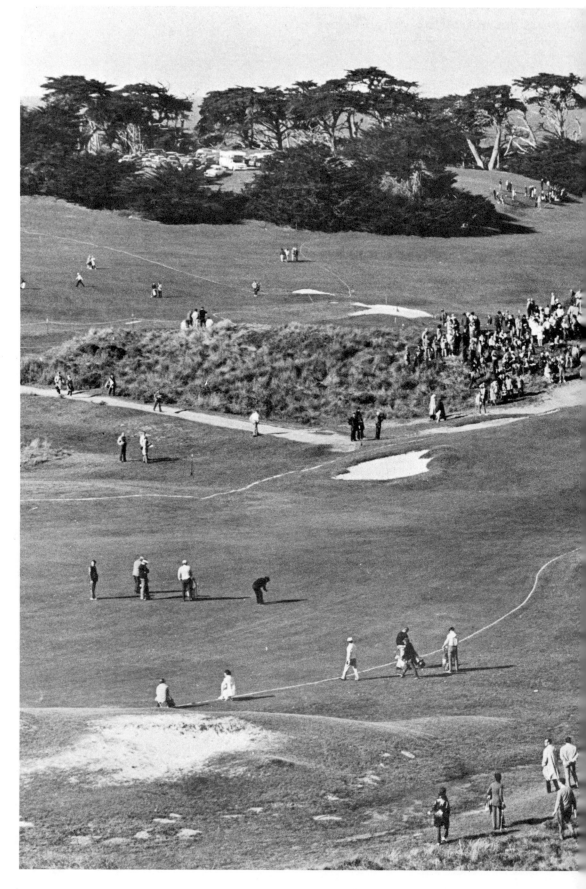

The rugged beauty of Cypress Point. A sweeping panorama of the 12th and 13th holes, progressing throug

the sand dunes to the wind-swept coast line.

Johnny Miller meets an admiring gallery of young deer on the 6th fairway of Cypress Point. The animals apparently were interested in a closer look at the fabled Miller swing.

asked Lunn. "For the birdie you're going to get here," replied LoPresti, feeling no pain. Lunn missed the green with his tee shot . . . and then chipped in for a deuce.

Among the Cypress members today are Bing Crosby and Bob Hope—Crosby listed on the men's handicap boards as an 8 and Hope as a 12. They belong to a flock of other clubs the world over, and rarely play Cypress anymore, but maintain a deep feeling of affection for it. "I guess I've gotten more publicity from one stroke I played there," says Crosby, "than any other shot I've ever hit."

That came in the late afternoon gloaming of an autumn day in 1947. Playing a fivesome with Henry Puget, Jack Morse, Harrison Goodwin and Dan Searle, Bing stood in the mist on the tee and pondered his options. He decided to go for the green with a driver, and hit the ball into the cup.

Henry Puget still lists that shot among his favorite memories in forty-one years as head pro at Cypress Point. Puget, who retired in 1972, was succeeded by Jim Langley, whose low-keyed approach blends perfectly with the Cypress tradition.

By far the most famous sequence of shots ever recorded at the 16th was the 16 strokes taken by Porky Oliver in the third round of the 1953 Crosby. Hitting into a fifty-mile-an-hour gale, Oliver put five shots into the ocean. He finally got over the water, but into the tangled ice plant. He chopped around until at length he holed out. Word spread fast, and when Oliver finished, there was a message waiting for him in the clubhouse—"call long-distance operator number 16."

In the later years, Porky would appreciate the recognition those 16 strokes afforded him, but at the time, contending for the championship, it was anything but humorous. Prescott Sullivan, the crusty San Francisco *Examiner* columnist, approached him that day with the remark, "That was priceless, Porky old boy. Best laugh we've had in years."

Oliver glared at him and snarled, "I guess you'd laugh at a broken leg."

Roger Kelly, a Los Angeles lawyer, was Oliver's amateur partner. "In my book Porky didn't make a bad shot among those sixteen," Kelly says. "But it's that kind of a hole."

Jack Burke won't argue that. For five straight years in the Crosby he came to the 16th tee under par for the day—and never finished the round. "He got shot down either by the ocean or the ice plant," says George Coleman, Burke's long-time amateur partner. Burke's pickups took him out of the individual pro competition, but he was able to continue in the pro-am division, thanks to Coleman getting a bogey on each occasion.

In 1957 Gardner Dickinson slashed his tee shot on 16 into the swirling waters. He took off his shoes, rolled up his slacks and waded in to have a few whacks at it. Gardner got the ball up over the cliff, finally, and putted out in bare feet for a 9.

Less persistent was Henry Ransom, who attempted a similar recovery and struck three shots directly into the cliff. The third one ricocheted back off the rocks and struck him in the stomach. Henry ordered his caddie to pick up the ball and stalked off angrily with the comment, "When they start hitting back at me, it's time to quit."

In the opening round of the 1975 Crosby, Raymond Floyd sauntered onto the 16th tee 3 under par. In the gallery were Bing and his wife, Kathy, and waiting on the tee was the next foursome, which included Johnny Miller, fresh from his record-setting triumphs in the Phoenix and Tucson tournaments. Floyd proceeded to line three straight iron shots into the rocks before getting across. His amateur partner, actor Clint Eastwood, tried the short cut to the plateau on the left and fell short. Miller was awe-struck. He picked out a 3-wood and hit it ten feet from the pin.

Cypress traditionally attracts the largest Crosby galleries on Thursday, when the celebrities play. Under the subtle caste system of the Crosby, the big names open at Cypress, move to Spyglass on Friday and then are assigned to Pebble Beach, where the television cameras are located. (It is ego-shattering to a celebrity to discover his Thursday round is scheduled either for Pebble Beach or Spyglass.)

The show business folk like to gather at Cypress to watch their colleagues. A spectator came into the Club XIX bar at Del Monte Lodge at noon, chuckling about the high winds. "They're making every woman look like Phyllis Diller out on 16," he said. The wind died down in the afternoon and the spectator returned to the 16th. He could find only one woman who looked like Phyllis Diller—and that was Phyllis Diller.

Joe Dey, the former executive director of the USGA and tour commissioner of the TPD, sums up the enchantment of Cypress Point. "If I were condemned to play only one course for the rest of my life," Dey said, "I would unhesitatingly pick Cypress Point."

One of golf's most scenic and demanding shots, from the 16th tee at Cypress. 33

In a scene framed beautifully by the majestic cypress trees and the narrow fairway chute, Jack Nicklaus putts from

the 18th green at Cypress Point.

A touch of urbanity amid the rugged natural beauty of the Spyglass Hill dunes. The upstairs bedrooms afford a g

ew of the 5th green.

Tom Watson driving from the 18th tee at Pebble Beach. The rocky coast line offers an inviting 2-stroke problem

errant hook.

The 6th at Pebble, approaching from the plateau far to the right of the fairway.

Ed (Porky) Oliver, one of the most popular Crosby regulars. Porky won the tournament in 1940, at Rancho Santa Fe.

Pebble Beach:
Nature's Masterpiece

Although it is frequented by the rich and often associated with a Social Register clientele, Pebble Beach is a public golf course. It is surely the most prominent public course in America, having fashioned its international reputation partially with its artful severity and partially with its natural beauty.

Catering primarily to the guests of Del Monte Lodge, Pebble Beach is open to the general public at $20 per round on week days and $30 on weekends, plus a $10 golf car fee. Over 36,000 rounds are played there annually.

Pebble Beach is, above all, a working

course. It held the U. S. Amateur in 1929, when it was won by Harrison R. (Jimmy) Johnston of Minneapolis with a shot off the receding waters of the beach along the 18th fairway; in 1947, when Skee Riegel outshot a strong field and again in 1961, when Jack Nicklaus won his second and last Amateur championship. In 1972 the U. S. Open finally came to Pebble Beach. It was a memorable tournament, won by Nicklaus with a score of 290, two strokes over par. Pebble has, in addition, held the California Amateur annually since 1919.

Ever since Crosby moved his tournament to the Monterey Peninsula in 1947, Pebble has been the anchor course. The final round is traditionally played there, and the network telecasts have made the closing holes as familiar to most American golf fans

as those at their own courses.

Pat Ward-Thomas of the Manchester *Guardian* in England has written:

The quality of the dramatic is the lasting impression of Pebble, and this is emphasized by its peaceful beginning which gives the stranger no hint of what is to come. There are many great finishing holes in golf, but none in my view can compare with the last at Pebble, that noble curve along the iron-bound shore. One can imagine the joy, and, too, the hint of malice there must have been in the hearts of Jack Neville and Douglas Grant when they saw what nature had presented them for their fashioning of a masterpiece.

A golfer from Edinburgh once came over to visit his good friend Peter Hay, the

Scottish-born pro at Pebble Beach for many years until his death. The Scot told Hay that he, the Scot, could not play the course. "It's too dommed beautiful," he burred. "I can't keep my mind on the game."

Hay understood. He is gone now, but his name is perpetuated by the lovely little par-3 course, named for him, at the entrance to Del Monte Lodge.

"Playing Pebble Beach is like fighting Rocky Marciano," Jack Burke observed twenty years ago. "Every time you step onto the course, you're a cinch to take a beating."

Time hasn't changed a thing. Today Burke could allude to Muhammad Ali instead of Marciano. Billy Farrell would agree. Farrell took 55 strokes on the first nine in the 1967 Crosby, before the round was washed out by a storm.

The course measures 6,343 yards from the regular tees and 6,815 yards from the championship tees, with ratings of 72 and 75. The competitive course record is 64—8 under par—by Rod Funseth in the 1972 Crosby.

"I doubt if many people realize what a fantastic score that was," says Art Bell, the Pebble Beach pro. Bell, a native of the Hawaiian Islands, is sixty-five, and he has seen just about every quality course in the United States. "Pebble is No. 1," Bell says. "It has every characteristic required of a great course."

The basic design Neville incorporated is roughly a figure 8. Beginning at the Del Monte Lodge, which overlooks Carmel Bay, the course moves inland for the first three holes, all rather modest in severity. The next seven holes, with the exception of the par-3 5th, move along the cliffs. From 11 through 16 the holes loop inland and then back to

Here's a competitor's view of the 8th green at Pebble, as seen from the crest of the cliff tops. Jack Nicklaus calls it the best second-shot hole in golf. The long-iron approach, from the edge of the cliff, must carry over the chasm and rocky shore to a bunker-framed green.

the water, finishing with the ocean very much in play on 17 and 18.

The course really begins on the 6th hole, an uphill par-5 that Byron Nelson considers the toughest of the eighteen. The next four holes are perched high atop a craggy spit that overhangs the ocean. The 7th is a tiny 110-yard downhill pitch, a soft wedge shot on calm days for the pros but a long iron into the gale. The 8th is one of the great two-shotters anywhere. After a blind drive to a plateau the approach must carry 180 to 190 yards, across the chasm that resembles a shark's maw, to a green surrounded by bunkers.

The 9th, 450 yards, and the 10th, 436 yards, stretch hard along the ocean. These are brutally difficult holes, under any conditions. Nicklaus nearly threw away his 1972 Open championship on the 10th, slicing a drive over the cliff down onto the beach below and taking a double bogey. Dale Douglass took a 19 on the hole in the 1963 Crosby.

In 1965 Tony Lema, the defending champion in the Crosby, was paired with Father John Durkin, a fine player who always showed up with a formidable handicap. As they stood on the 8th tee, Lema turned to the priest and said, "Partner, you will have to get bogeys on these next three holes, and with your strokes we'll get out alive. There is no way I can par them all."

The remaining holes are scarcely easier. In the final round of the 1967 Crosby, Arnold Palmer was one stroke behind Nicklaus when he came to the 14th, a 555-yard par-5. Attempting to reach the green with his second, Palmer hit a mighty 3-wood that ticked the branches of a tree on the right and caromed out of bounds. Arnold

hit the tree with his next shot, and that one also landed OB. He took 9 on the hole and finished third, behind Nicklaus and Billy Casper.

That night a storm struck Pebble Beach, and when the grounds crew went out the next morning to survey the damage, they discovered the tree had been uprooted and blown to the ground.

Johnny Miller led Nicklaus by a stroke on the final round of the 1972 Crosby as they walked together down the 16th fairway. "I can't say that I've played very well, Jack," Miller said. "It's taken me 69 holes to figure my problem out. But I've got it corrected now." On his next shot, a 7-iron, Miller shanked the ball. He wound up in a tie with Nicklaus, and lost to Jack's birdie on the first play-off hole.

Jack Burke and George Coleman appeared to have the pro-am wrapped up in 1971 until Coleman 4-putted the 17th green, enabling Lou Graham and Father Durkin to win. The priest had a momentary twinge of conscience over his handicap,

then 17. "I'm expecting a wire from the Vatican any day," he said, "asking for a review of my handicap."

No golfer has ever been more vividly associated with disaster on any one hole than Palmer on the 17th at Pebble Beach. It wiped him out two years in succession.

A rugged, 218-yard hole requiring anything from a long iron to a driver, the 17th runs toward the ocean to a green flanked by rocks and the Pacific. In the third round of the 1963 Crosby, Palmer's 2-iron shot sailed over the green and disappeared, apparently into the water.

Invoking the lost-ball rule, Arnold hit another from the tee. His first ball was found lying in the rocks on the beach, however, and so he played that onto the green. Following the completion of the tournament the next day, PGA officials, in a review of the situation, decided that Palmer had struck an unauthorized provisional ball—that he, in effect, had abandoned his first ball by hitting the second. He was disqualified, even

Palmer on the Rocks. Arnold struggles to his famous 9 on the par-3 No. 17 at Pebble Beach in the 1964 Crosby (left). In the photo above, the 17th green is in the lower right, with the 18th fairway stretching majestically along the water.

though he had played the fourth round, and his string of 47 consecutive tournaments in the money was over.

The next year, the 17th at Pebble, served as the scene for the famous "Palmer on the Rocks" incident, resulting in a 9 for Arnold and seventeen minutes of memorable footage for the television cameras. It occurred, again, on the third round.

Palmer hit his tee shot over the cliff behind the green, into shallow water in front of the 18th tee. The bay and its beaches were then played as "part of the course," meaning that a golfer could not take a lateral water penalty stroke (the local rule was later abolished and the beaches are now regarded as a water hazard).

Palmer stood there, with a stray dog watching him curiously, and flailed away at the ball. Jimmy Demaret was working the tournament as a roving television commentator. Observing Palmer's predicament, Demaret pointed out the options under the unplayable ball rule. He reported that Palmer could lift and drop, keeping the line behind the position of the ball. "In that case," remarked Demaret, "his nearest drop would be Honolulu." Palmer continued to play it off the rocks.

Jim Murray of the Los Angeles *Times*, staring wryly at the scene from the vantage point of his living-room television set, described it in this manner:

"Palmer . . . was so far out on a moor in the ocean he looked like Robinson Crusoe. His only companions were a dog and a sand wedge. I thought for a minute we had switched channels and Walt Disney was bringing us another of those heart-warming stories of a boy and his dog, but a companion, peering closely had a better idea: 'Shouldn't that dog have a cask around his neck?' "

In contrast to Palmer's woes on the 17th is the historic shot struck on the 18th in 1952 by an amateur, Billy Hoelle, then employed as a salesman for Bing Crosby's Minute Maid orange juice firm.

Hoelle and his partner, Art Bell, trailed the pro-am leaders, Bob Toski and Dr. Bob Knudson, by 4 shots on the 17th tee. Bell dropped a long birdie putt on 17, then on 18 Hoelle chopped an 8-iron shot out of a wet sand trap into the cup for a net 2, a double eagle. The 2–2 finish earned Bell and Hoelle a share of the pro-am championship with Toski and Knudson.

"It was a million-to-one shot," groaned Crosby, whose Calcutta money had been on the Toski team.

The incident which best symbolizes the capricious qualities of Pebble Beach occurred in 1965. A San Francisco amateur, Matt Palacio, hit his drive on the 18th in the general direction of China and muttered, "Only God can save that one." The waves suddenly receded, the ball struck a bare rock, and it caromed back onto a favorable spot on the fairway. Palacio gazed up at the heavens and mumbled, "Thank you, God."

It remained for Mason Rudolph, the touring philosopher from Clarksville, Tennessee, to analyze Pebble Beach. After a particularly rugged round in the 1972 Open, Mason smiled weakly and said, "This course is built right around my game. Unfortunately, it touches no part of it."

THE
SHOW

The Evolution of a Classic

On the American sporting scene today only a handful of events can be classified as institutions, or, to employ a more contemporary term, happenings. The Kentucky Derby comes to mind, along with Forest Hills and the Indianapolis 500.

These events are week-long gatherings of watchers who often contribute as much to the flavor of the show as the competition itself. People come to see and be seen, and they come from all strata of our society.

Bing Crosby's National Pro-Am has evolved into a socioeconomic sports spectacular of this rare order.

It originated, curiously enough, as a casual weekend of fun for Bing and his friends. The first Crosby, in 1937 at Rancho Santa Fe near San Diego, didn't even have Bing's name on it. The tournament was born as the Rancho Santa Fe Amateur-Pro, the hyphenated designation disclosing where the pros stood in those days.

The format called for 36 holes of competition for the pro-amateur teams and a purse of $3,000. On hand from the tour,

such as it was then, were Henry Picard, Leonard Dodson, Denny Shute, Paul Runyan, Lloyd Mangrum, Olin Dutra, Dutch Harrison, Willie Goggin, Johnny Revolta and a rustic product of the West Virginia hills, Sam Snead.

The official amateur list included Richard Arlen, Zeppo Marx, Edgar Kennedy, Guy Kibbee, Bill Frawley, Fred Astaire, Andy Clyde and Jimmy McLarnin, but most of them showed up just for the parties and didn't bother to tee up.

Also on the scene, incongruously enough, was the shadowy John ("Mysterious")

Montague, a golf hustler who once beat Bing by playing with only a baseball bat, shovel and rake. Montague was often just a half step ahead of the law, and there was widespread speculation whether he would risk the publicity of actually entering the tournament.

On the evening before the scheduled opening round, Lawson Little threw a cocktail party at the Del Mar Hotel for Montague and other guests. Bob Myers, Los Angeles bureau sports editor of the Associated Press, began pressing Montague for confirmation of his entry.

It was raining hard, the liquor was flowing and soon Myers, who had been a top amateur boxer in Texas at one time, challenged Montague. "Tell me whether or not you're going to play," Myers said, "or put up your fists and fight." Myers swung a mighty left hook, Montague turned away just in time, and the punch caught Lawson Little squarely on the left eye. Montague, shaken by the incident, admitted he had no intention of playing.

Rain washed away the first round, and that night Crosby approached Fred Corcoran, the new tournament director of the PGA, with the $3,000 check. "Take it and distribute the money any way you want," Bing said. "We'll never be able to play tomorrow."

Corcoran advised him to wait, and the next day the sun came out. The golf course was a bog, but Snead went out and shot 68 to win by four strokes. When Bing presented Sam with his first-place check of $500, Sam stalled a few moments and then allegedly replied, "If you don't mind, Mr. Crosby, I'd rather have cash." Sam can't recall the statement, but Bing claims it's true.

Bing brought the tournament back the

In a page torn out of the past, a long-ago Crosby foursome of Dan Searle, Cam Puget, Bing and Jimmy Demaret stride resolutely through the Cypress Point dune lands.

next year, expanding his role as host. He set up little bars in the back yard of his home near the golf course. Steaks were grilled for the contestants, and Bing broke into a few ballads. The stag party was crashed by a group of Hollywood starlets, to no one's serious concern.

"Everything was pretty informal at the Crosby in those days," recalls Bob Gardner, an amateur from Los Angeles. "Our entry fee was $3. Maurie Luxford, the starter, would collect it on the first tee. If he missed you one day, he'd catch you the next."

When Ed Lowery made a last-minute withdrawal from the 1938 tournament, his place was filled out by Fred Corcoran, who had no golf clubs. The pros loaned him some, and Corcoran went to the first tee with a set that included six wedges.

The tournament died out at Rancho after the war year of 1942 and was revived at Monterey in 1947. Originally it was to be only at Pebble Beach, but Crosby conceived the idea of holding it over three courses —Pebble Beach, Cypress Point and the Monterey Peninsula Country Club.

Joe Novak, president of the California PGA, advised Bing there was no precedent on the U.S. tour for using three courses for the same tournament. Unconvinced, Crosby tracked down Fred Corcoran, who was dining at the Pen and Pencil restaurant in New York. "They hold the British Open on more than one course," Corcoran told him. "I see no reason why you can't."

So the tournament arrived at Monterey in 1947 with a purse of $10,000, which Bing paid out of his own pocket. Gross receipts were just over $9,000, and the money, after expenses, was contributed to area charities.

Once established, the Crosby underwent subtle transformations. The purse escalated almost annually. Network television covered the tournament in 1958, and competition was expanded from 54 to 72 holes.

The show business people have continued to play, but some of the old atmosphere of fun and conviviality has become noticeably less pervasive, particularly among the more serious-minded pros. No longer can they say that the Crosby has more parties than pars.

"Until they went to 72 holes," remarked Jimmy Demaret, who enjoys a good time, "the entire field played the game course each day. You'd see everybody. When they started playing three courses the same day, it took some of the closeness out of the tournament."

For pros like Cary Middlecoff, however, the Crosby still offered the best times on the tour. "I enjoyed playing with the celebrities," says Middlecoff, who won the Crosby in 1955 and 1956. "It was a good place for a star-struck young pro like myself to meet them. I rubbed noses with them all."

Yet when Middlecoff returned to the Crosby as a television commentator in 1966, after an absence of nearly a decade, he observed one startling change. "Most of us used to stay at the same hotel in downtown Monterey, the Casa Munras," he said. "When you went into the hotel bar at night, you'd know almost everybody there. By 1966 the players were scattered, and one day I found out why. On the way to the golf course I drove by blocks and blocks of new motels which weren't even there ten years earlier."

One of the most salient victims of progress has been the Clambake, the traditional tournament dinner party. For years it was held on Sunday night at the

Sam Snead, when he had a full head of hair. Resplendent in white shirt and tie, Sam surveys a putt during the 1938 Crosby at Rancho Santa Fe.

conclusion of the competition, at the Monterey Peninsula Country Club. Bing served as master of ceremonies and awarded the checks to the pros. Lionel Hebert contributed a trumpet solo, and Jimmy Demaret joined Bing for a few songs. The "official" entertainers included show business people like Rosemary Clooney, Phil Harris, Jimmy Durante and Bing's brother, Bob.

But the pros, eager to move on to the next tournament, stopped showing up. Bing moved the Clambake to Wednesday night at the Monterey County Fairgrounds in 1962, changing its format to a reward dinner for the hundreds of volunteer workers. It lost the old flavor, and Crosby old-timers were remembering wistfully the times like 1957, when a storm lashed the peninsula just after the tournament had finished. The power supply was cut off, and the guests dined jovially by candlelight. The bartenders cheerfully mixed drinks, as columnist Prescott Sullivan put it, "by memory."

But the tournament continued to grow, the television ratings climbed along with the purses, and the galleries turned out in record numbers. In 1975 the gross receipts were nearly $600,000, largest in Crosby history. The tournament pays $2,000 rent annually to each of the three courses, and finances the clean-up work.

The Crosby influence on the tournament has been enormous. "Most people in golf have no idea how immensely significant the Crosby format has been in making tournament golf big business," says golf historian Herb Graffis. "Bob Harlow and Fred Corcoran did a tremendous job of pioneering it, then Bing came along at the right time with the right idea. When he got

that Youth Fund as beneficiary, he caught charity lightning in a bottle.

"Nobody was talking about golfing millionaires at that time. Bing was aware they needed tournaments and needed sponsors. He knew the golfers, inside their heads and hearts, and he knew the show crowd. After all, he had been around in those Great Gatsby days when the hardest shot in golf was trying to get a ball out of Paul Whiteman's footprints in the sand."

Bob Hope was talking recently about the special flavor of the Crosby. "There's a lot of sentiment for Bing's tournament," Hope said. "He was the pioneer, the guy who started all these celebrity awards. I take a lot of pride in my own tournament, but we should all remember that Bing's was the first."

Happy times at the Clambake (above left) for Lloyd Mangrum, Dean Martin, Phil Harris, Don Cherry, Jimmy Demaret and Jimmy Thomson. (Below left) Fred Corcoran gags it up as an arbiter between two mythical rivals.

Bing: The Perfect Host

Sipping tea one recent afternoon in the library of his home in Hillsborough, California, Bing Crosby was asked what single accomplishment—movie, gold record or whatever—had given him the most satisfaction throughout his long career.

"The golf tournament," he replied quickly. "No doubt about that. It's been hard work for a lot of people, but so much good has been done from it. It's certainly the thing I'd most like to be remembered for."

Bing has been associated with golf in one form or another since he first began caddying at the Spokane Country Club in 1916 for $.50 a round.

Curiously enough, Bing originally had no intention of getting into show business. He was taking a pre-law course at Gonzaga University in Spokane, his home town, and working part time in the paymaster's office of a railroad company to pay his school expenses.

"One day I glanced at the check that was going to the head attorney of the railroad," Bing recalled. "I figured if that was the best I had to look forward to, I'd be better off in some other business. So I started singing with some local bands, and that led to the job with Pops Whiteman."

After joining the Whiteman band, as the lead singer in "The Rhythm Boys," Bing had free time in the afternoons to work on his game. He became a member of the Lakeside Club in Hollywood in 1931, got his handicap down to 2, and won the Lakeside championship five times. He competed in the 1940 U.S. and 1950 British amateurs.

Crosby married actress Dixie Lee, settled in the Holmby Hills district of Hollywood and raised four sons—Gary, Dennis, Phillip and Lindsay. He maintained his Lakeside membership and also joined Bel-Air, where he began playing a considerable amount of golf with Bob Gardner, who had participated in a couple of Bing's earlier tournaments at Rancho Santa Fe.

"One day we came in off the course for a drink in the locker room," Gardner recalled. "Bing asked me how my classes were going at UCLA, where I had enrolled after getting out of the service. I told him fine, except that I was having trouble finding a place to live.

"He excused himself for a few minutes to make a phone call. 'I just talked to Dixie,' he told me. 'It's all set. We've got a spare room and you can stay with us as long as you want.' I lived there for the next three years."

It was an indelible experience for Gardner.

"Bing got along with all types of

Armed with knickers, sweater, pipe and umbrella, Bing, as ever, is the inimitable host. An umbrella is standard equipment in the regulation Crosby survival kit.

people," he says. "He knew a little bit about everything. He could talk politics or show business or sports with presidents of companies or caddies.

"But God, how he hated to lose on the golf course! He would do anything to win. If he had me down at the turn and I asked for more strokes, he would just say, 'Get out the way you got in.' If I beat him, he'd suggest an extra four-hole Whiskey Route—playing the first, second, eighth and ninth holes. If he was out of the match after sixteen holes, he rigged up a special press he called the Railroad Route—$5 nassaus on 17 and 18. He generally got his money back."

Bing's most celebrated show business friendships have been with Bob Hope and Phil Harris, and they are genuine. "I had a lot of fun making those *Road* pictures with Hope," Crosby says. "We filmed everything right in Hollywood, the jungle scenes and all. Never had to go on location. I used to tee off at Lakeside at six in the morning, play eighteen holes and report to the set at nine. I've enjoyed traveling and working with Phil, too, except that I never could match him with the bottle."

One of the first stipulations Crosby made when he started his golf tournament, a regulation that has continued through the years with the exception of a special exemption granted to Francis Brown, was that everybody walked; no golf cars allowed. Hope used to chide him about that, and when Bob launched his own tournament at Palm Springs in 1960, he allowed the use of golf cars.

"Hope draws an older crowd for his little party," Bing chuckled.

The last time Bing played in his own tournament was 1956, when he was paired with Ben Hogan. They led the pro-am the first day with a 60 at Cypress Point. "After that," Hogan recalls, "Bing continued to play very well and I played very badly." It was six months after Ben had lost his bid for a fifth U. S. Open championship in a play-off with Jack Fleck at the Olympic Club in San Francisco. His legs, shattered in his 1949 automobile accident, were aching. The rain was pouring down as Crosby and Hogan approached the 13th hole on the final round at Pebble Beach, where Bing then owned a home.

"Ben, if you'd like to pack it in right here, let's quit and have a drink in my house," Crosby told him. Hogan fixed that familiar gaze of arctic blue on his old friend. "If you don't mind, Bing," he said, "I'd rather play it out."

Crosby nodded. "Let's play," he said.

Hogan finished the round with an 81.

By that time Crosby was a widower. He had met a young starlet in Hollywood named Kathy Grant, and on their first date over dinner, Kathy asked him about his hobbies.

"Oh, I like to hunt and fish a little," Bing replied. "And of course there's the golf tournament."

"What tournament?"

"The Crosby, at Pebble Beach."

"Ummm. Oh, yes." Kathy had never heard of it.

They were married in 1957, and have three children—Harry, Mary Frances, the only Crosby daughter, and Nathaniel. "Mary Frances is 15, going on 24," says Bing. "She's got her mother's looks, that's for sure."

Kathy Crosby discovered quickly enough her husband's deep personal involvement in the tournament. "He selects the amateur players," she says. "The toughest thing he has to do is say no to the thousands of people who want to play. I've seen him sweat and worry for days before calling someone to say he wasn't being invited this time. It's a very personal thing for Bing."

The tournament field has 168 amateurs, and Bing tries to shuffle the entries to include 50 new players each year from an application list which surpassed 9,000 last year. "I know the problem," says Bob Hope. "I go through it myself. When you sponsor a tournament, you don't just lend your name. It's the time and the effort and the realization that you have to say no to so many nice people."

Bing has received some classic requests. Once a man wrote and said that

Kathy Crosby, John Daly and Bing on the steps of Del Monte Lodge. At right, Larry Crosby, the man behind the tournament for nearly forty years until his death in 1975. Bing (opposite page) strikes a snappy pose with the pretty scorekeepers. The ladies are a popular feature at the Crosby.

he had suffered two heart attacks, and his next one would be fatal it he didn't get a chance to play in the tournament. Bing put him in, with a note saying that a guy with his heart condition really shouldn't be playing those tough courses.

Art Rosenbaum, sports editor and columnist of the San Francisco *Chronicle*, tells another story:

"A friend of mine in the East was sweating out his invitation. The deadline passed, and still no letter. He was having trouble with his wife at the time, and one night they became involved in a bitter wrangle. The woman, in a supreme moment of retribution, admitted she had thrown the invitation into the fireplace a week earlier. The man reached for the phone, called his lawyer and initiated divorce proceedings."

During the tournament, the Crosbys move into a little apartment on the second floor of the clubhouse at Cypress Point, with a view of the 16th tee from one corner and the 18th green from another. Bing likes to mingle with the galleries, usually near the 15th green at Cypress or on the promontory point near the 6th green and 7th tee at Pebble Beach. He is ever aware who he is and what he is, but greets everyone warmly and is very much a part of the flavor of his tournament.

"Bing has a sense of folksy erudition," says Art Rosenbaum, "of being someone above the masses, yet a neighbor among them."

Going for 3 the hard way. Bing on the 16th at Cypress. He aced the hole in 1947 during a social round.

Curtain call for Ben Hogan and Bing in the 1956 Crosby. It was the last competitive appearance in the tournament for each. They teamed as partners, and led the pro-am at Cypress with a 60.

Crosby turned seventy-one in 1975, and his stage is emptying. Peter Hay died in 1961, Samuel Morse in 1969, Maurie Luxford in 1971 and then, in February of 1975, Bing's brother Larry succumbed to cancer. Larry was his business associate for forty years and the general manager of the Crosby tournament. He also was Bing's friend.

One day Father Len Scannell had just finished his practice round at Pebble Beach and asked Bing, waiting for him on the 18th green, if there was anything he could do.

"Well, yes, Father, there is," Crosby said. "It looks like we're going to get rain. You might put in a word with the man upstairs for some good weather."

Father Scannell smiled and replied, "That's out of my department, Bing. I'm in sales, not management."

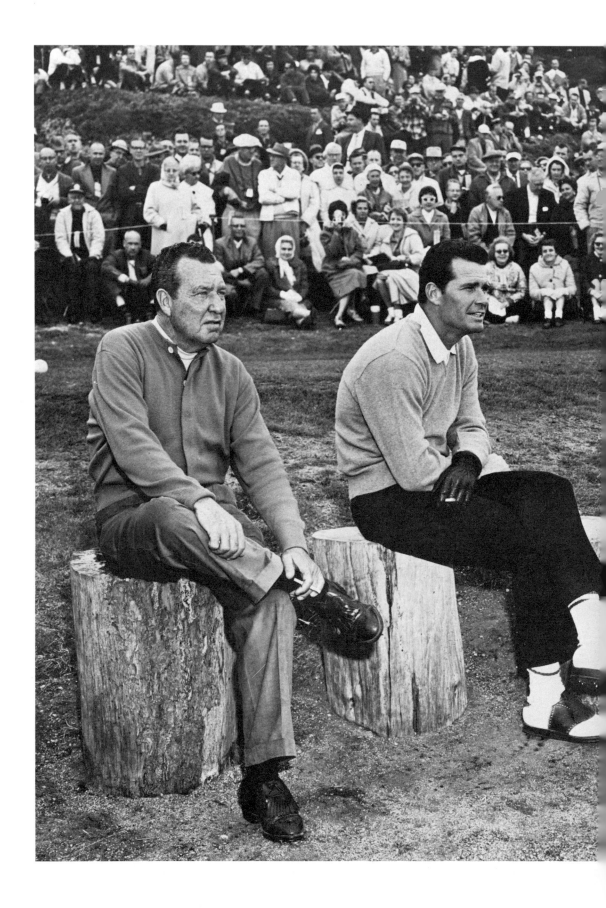

Caught in a rare moment of relaxation, Phil Harris, Jim Garner and Arnold Palmer take a cigaret break. Something, or someone, has obviously caught their eye.

The Celebrities: Slapstick and Melodrama

Trumpeter Harry James shuffled disconsolately off the 18th tee at Pebble Beach a few years ago. Harry and his pro partner were 18 over par for the day, reason enough to be dejected, but the gallery was giggling loudly. The scoreboard boy, in a moment of presumed confusion, had inverted the figures to read 81 over par.

"Never mind," snickered Phil Harris. "By the time they finish they won't have to change that board."

Show business celebrities have been a flavorful feature of the Crosby from the onset, seldom playing with distinction but invariably providing glamour appeal and comic relief for the paying customers and television viewers.

Among the most durable entries has been Phil Harris, the boulevardier whose friendship with Crosby traces back to 1925. A radio legend as the tipsy bandleader on the Jack Benny show, Harris did not start playing golf until the late 1940s. "I was too busy drinking," he says. He surfaced at the Crosby for the first time in 1951 and was a participating regular until 1975 when, at the age of seventy, he decided to hang up his spikes and confine his contributions to being the self-proclaimed tournament "social director."

Harris never became an accomplished golfer. He was an 8-handicapper briefly in the 1950s, but a chronic slice brought that up to 16 in later years, and he was comfortable with it. "I finally cured the slice," Harris said last year. "I quit playing."

In his maiden appearance at the Crosby, in 1951, Harris teamed with Dutch Harrison to win the pro-am. The clinching stroke was a birdie putt by Harris on the 17th at Pebble Beach. Nobody has ever really determined the exact distance of the putt, various estimates ranging from 60 to 90 feet. It was by any standard a classic, negotiating a double break over the hourglass-shaped green, and as the ball disappeared into the cup, Harris threw his putter into the air and cried, "You take it in from here, Dutch." Phil walked in and let his partner get the clinching par on the home hole.

Asked at the Clambake that night if the putt really did cover 90 feet, Harris snorted and replied, "Hell, it broke that much."

Determined to get the exact distance of the putt, several writers approached George (Scorpie) Doyle, Phil's caddie. "I can't say for sure," Scorpie declared, "but I'd like to have that much footage along Wilshire Boulevard."

There was a serious sequel to the incident. Scorpie Doyle, at the time, had a drinking problem. Harris, a bottle man himself, offered the caddie a deal. He would give Scorpie his share of the pro-am prize and Calcutta money if the caddie would promise never to take another drink. Phil then arranged with Ben Hogan, at the time the pro at Tamarisk Country Club in Palm Desert, to give Doyle a job. Today Scorpie Doyle is the club starter at Tamarisk, a sober and respected man. He owes his life, literally, to the pledge he made Phil Harris.

Phil himself never felt compelled to go on the wagon. He built a profitable image as a drinker, as Dean Martin has. One year Harris and Crosby were traveling together through Scotland by car. Bing was driving, and as they passed the lights of a distillery on the way to their motel after a night of drinking, Crosby nudged his pal and said, "Look over there, Phil. They're makin' it faster than you can drink it."

Harris opened his eyes, yawned and said, "Yeah, but at least I got the bastards working nights."

In a recent Crosby, Harris, paired in a

group with Dean Martin, staggered to the first tee at Spyglass. He whiffed his first swing, then whiffed another.

"Don't stop now," cracked Martin. "You've got a no-hitter going."

"I'm not a drunk," insisted Harris after finishing the round. "A drunk is a guy with yellow tennis shoes and a rusty zipper."

Harris plays no favorites with his jibes. Anyone is fair game. Approaching the 8th green at Cypress Point one morning, he noticed the groundskeeper leaning on a tall rake. "Hey, fella," Phil shouted. "You take my driver and I'll use your rake."

When Crosby was hospitalized with a lung infection during the 1974 tournament, Harris filled in for him as television commentator in the tower overlooking the 18th green at Pebble Beach. Chris Schenkel, the perfect straight man, observed that Johnny Miller had just hit a bunker shot with a smooth touch.

"Yeah," agreed Harris into the microphone. "As smooth as a man lifting a breast out of an evening gown."

"I was under such heavy sedation that week I hardly remember anything about watching the tournament on TV," Bing said. "But that remark from Phil woke me up."

A few minutes later Schenkel identified Gay Brewer walking up the 18th fairway. Harris was ready. "Gay Brewer? I always thought he was a little fag wine maker from Modesto."

In his later years Phil was often paired with the irascible Dave Hill. Harris was fond of provoking Hill's short fuse. On the 16th hole at Pebble Beach, Hill hit his approach shot into a trap. Harris, noting that the ball was buried in the footprints of a woman's high heel mark, called his partner over and suggested some form of retribution. "Good

idea," snapped Hill. "I'm gonna find that woman and brand her."

"I'll help you," cried Harris, grabbing his wedge and plunging into the gallery.

Andy Williams, another Crosby perennial, traces his association with Bing back to the hit record "Swingin' on a Star" that Williams and his three brothers cut with Bing a number of years ago. "It was the only gold record I've ever made," Andy says, "and we did it for scale. I got $25."

Andy was thirteen at the time.

In 1968 Williams began sponsoring his own tour event, at San Diego, "The course, Torrey Pines, is quite difficult," he says, "but nothing like what you face at the Crosby. The only way I can carry the 16th at Cypress Point is with a full driver and a hundred-mile-an-hour wind at my back."

A dapper man with no real athletic background, Williams is a golfer of modest skills. He carries a 14 handicap at Bel-Air in Los Angeles, and admits he can't play to it in the Crosby. He was Bert Yancey's partner in 1970, the year Yancey won the Crosby, but the two missed the pro-am cut.

One of the all-time favorites of the Crosby galleries is Tennessee Ernie Ford. He lives in Portola Valley, less than twenty minutes from Bing's residence in Hillsborough, and has been on the Crosby firing line for sixteen years.

Ford was walking off the 18th at Spyglass in a recent Crosby when a middle-aged woman rushed up to him. "You don't know me, Tennessee," she said, "but last year on the 14th hole at Pebble Beach you hit a nice shot to the green. After you walked away, I went out and picked up the divot. I took it back and planted it in my garden. It's still there."

On the 13th hole at Cypress Point the

Film stars are always a part of the Crosby scene. In the top photo, Johnny Weissmuller, the old movie Tarzan, takes a mighty swat. Below, Randolph Scott cools off with an orange juice offered by a Minute Maid miss.

Glen Campbell (above) silhouetted against the Pacific. Raymond Floyd and Clint Eastwood form a tight partnership in the bottom photo at left, and at bottom right, a pensive Andy Williams.

next year, Ford, a 15-handicapper who hits a good many low, hard shots, skulled a wedge that skipped over the green. It struck a lady squarely on the shin and caromed back six feet from the cup. Ford got his par, then walked over to apologize to the woman and inspect the bruise. "Don't worry, Ernie," she gushed, "it's my souvenir from watching you play. I hope it never goes away."

Clint Eastwood is not only a ranking celebrity in the Crosby, but also a local boy. He lives in Del Monte Forest, sponsors a tennis tournament annually at Pebble Beach and owns a large chunk of real estate in Carmel Valley. Eastwood remembers his first exposure to the Crosby in 1952.

"I was in the Army, stationed at Fort Ord," he says. "They held the Crosby Clambake, the big tournament dinner, on Sunday night at the Monterey Peninsula Country Club. An Army buddy and I crashed that party. We claimed we were assistants for Art Rosenbaum, the San Francisco writer. They let us in. I had the best steak I'd ever tasted, and then I went around and ate up all the left-over desserts."

Years later Eastwood, by then a television star in "Rawhide," appeared on a TV talk show in Salinas with people who were playing in the Crosby. Asked if he were in the tournament, Clint replied, "No, I'm not. I guess they don't like cowboys."

Soon after he received an invitation for the next Crosby. On it was a note from Larry Crosby, Bing's brother, with the words, "By the way, we do like cowboys."

Eastwood plays to an 18 handicap, exactly double the figure proudly carried by Dean Martin. Dino, for all his reputed excesses, is a strong player. Golfers at Riviera claim that if you get into a nassau game with Martin, you'd better hang onto your wallet.

But Dino's thirst is no myth. Walking in off the 18th at Pebble Beach one day, he was asked by Art Spander of the San Francisco *Chronicle* for a capsule size-up of his round.

"I didn't get a par until the fifth hole," Dino said. "Then I brought out the vodka. I played great the rest of the way. Those Russians have all the answers."

Actor Jim Garner is one of the best golfers in the show biz crowd, a 3 at Riviera. He has shot a 79 at Cypress Point, with birdies on 17 and 18. The thing he remembers most about the Crosby, though, is hitting an approach shot on the 16th at Pebble Beach that landed in the lap of a woman sitting on a stool near the green.

"I played it almost perfect," Garner claims. "If the woman hadn't been there, it would have glanced off the mound near the bunker and right onto the green."

The next night Garner was enjoying a quiet dinner in the Del Monte Lodge with Father John Durkin. A middle-aged woman—not the one who had been in the way of his ball—tottered over to their table, obviously full of martinis. She began berating Garner for no apparent reason. Garner said nothing. Father Durkin turned to the woman and said, "Lady, why don't you just leave?" That triggered another verbal onslaught at the film star, who still remained silent. Finally the woman staggered away.

Garner smiled at the priest and said, "Father, you really know how to get a guy in trouble."

For a man whose knees and back are wracked with injuries from football and auto accidents, Garner is an exceptionally good

It's a long day for cigar-chewing Jack Lemmon (above). Bob Stack hits an untouchable shot (right) and Lefty O'Doul, Jackie Jensen and Allie Reynolds exchange baseball gossip (below).

player and an intense competitor. "The worse the weather gets, the better chance I have to score," he says. "The wind and the rain eliminate the high handicapper right away. He can't handle the elements.

"I think the Crosby galleries are among the best in golf, but they do have one strange characteristic. They'll laugh when an amateur makes a bad shot. A pro knocks one in the ocean, and they sympathize with him. When I do it, they think it's funny. It's costing my pro money and I'm doing the best I can, and I get hot when the gallery yaks it up when I skull one."

Another first-class player is Glen Campbell, who followed the example of Crosby, Hope and Williams in sponsoring his own tournament, the Los Angeles Open. He did not play golf in his home town of Delight, Arkansas, but took up the game when he moved to Los Angeles in 1960 and eventually got down to a 2 handicap.

"The biggest thrill of my life would be if Bobby Nichols and I won the pro-am in Bing's tournament," Campbell says. "I'm not sure it will ever happen. I seem to have a jinx.

"One year Bobby and I played Pebble on Saturday, the third round, and shot 11 under par. The next day, with a good chance to win, we were 1 over."

The following year Glen played a practice round at Cypress Point in 72, even par. The next day, opening the tournament at Cypress, he shot 86.

And that brings us to Jack Lemmon, who has clowned and gagged his way through a decade of Crosby "competition." One pro suggested Lemmon should be arrested for impersonating a golfer. It has been said his backswing is shorter than his cigar.

Lemmon carries a 16-handicap at Hillcrest in Los Angeles, but generally he uses up most of that on the first nine in the Crosby. He is awed by the game and those who play it well. "I have an incredible feeling of respect for the touring pros," he says. "I'm a sports buff anyway, but golf is something special. You're alone out there. You get no help from a teammate passing the ball.

"I don't play very well, but it doesn't really bother me. Golf's not my bag. If I went out and blew my lines and screwed up a scene at work, then I'm going to be very deeply upset. But not in a golf tournament, and certainly not at the Crosby, where everybody has a good time anyway."

Lemmon first became interested in the Crosby when he was working on a picture at Columbia called *Operation Mad Ball* with Kathy Grant, who was then dating Bing. Invited to play in the tournament the next year, he arrived to discover a message saying the caddie he had hired couldn't make it.

"I looked around the caddie pen for a replacement," Lemmon says, "and this fellow, an older guy with a big, heavy overcoat, comes up and says he'd like the job. I learned later he was one of the great lushes of all time, but at this minute he was sober.

"I'm playing Spyglass the first round, with an 8:46 tee time. At eight o'clock I pick him up at Pebble in a little compact car I had rented and we drive over to Spyglass. His breath is so strong my eyes start to water. He's smashed at 8 A.M.

"Well, on the first tee I hit a pretty good 3-wood, take a bow for the gallery and start walking down the fairway, still carrying that 3-wood. I'm on top of the world. I look around—and my caddie is gone. He's searching for my bag. Lost it on the first tee. Finally he finds it and comes rumbling down the fairway, lurching and stumbling. About a hundred yards off the tee, on a piece of perfectly flat ground, he slips, my clubs fly out of the bag and he's flat on his ass.

"On the second hole I hear this tinkling, like jingle bells. I don't know what it is. The sun comes out and off comes that big coat, hitting the ground like a ten-ton rock. He had pint bottles stashed away in the lining, four or five of them clanking together on the bottom."

Lemmon's devotion to the Crosby is relentless. "I've done everything short of committing mayhem to play," he says. "I've juggled motion picture schedules and shuffled production deadlines and whatever else needed so I could clear that week. One year I just got myself locked in. No way I could play. I wrote Bing a letter, which turned out to be almost a book, apologizing because I couldn't come up. It means that much to me."

That feeling is shared by Jack's good friend, actor Bob Stack. "The Crosby is the only tournament I know where you can't buy your way in," Stack says. "Either Bing invites you or he doesn't. Everyone pays his entry fee, including all the celebrities. That's a rarity in pro-ams, too.

"It's never easy for a celebrity to play reasonably well in Bing's tournament. With those big galleries, it's like a zoo syndrome. They come out to watch the dancing bear. And I know those courses will eat me up; they always do.

"Last year I was trying to get my game halfway decent for the Crosby. I was practicing at Bel-Air, my home club, and the pro, Eddie Merrins, came out to watch for a few minutes. He asked me which one of my 13 swings I would use this year."

Dean Martin, a solid 8 from Riviera. Dino's bar talk occasionally shrouds the fact he is a strong player, very much at home on the tough Crosby courses.

Bob Hope: Road to Repartee

Of all the assorted characters from vaudeville, movies, radio, television, politics and other fields Crosby has imported through the years for his tournament, no one symbolizes the spirit of the event more than Leslie Townes Hope.

Bob Hope played in the tournament for the first time in 1939, two years after he fled Broadway to make his home in California. He continued to appear almost annually until 1965, and for many spectators, oblivious to the talents of a Lloyd Mangrum or a Julius Boros, Hope was the feature attraction.

He provided such a torrent of gags that many overlooked his exceptional playing ability. The years have taken their toll on Hope's distance, and today he plays to a modest 14 handicap, but in his prime he was a solid 6 with a deadly putting stroke Crosby claims was learned on pool tables during his youth.

Hope's greatest moment in the Crosby—on the course—was at the 14th hole at Pebble Beach during the last round of the 1952 tournament. He and his pro partner, Jimmy Demaret, were one stroke off the pro-am team lead going into that eminently hazardous 555-yard hole that doglegs right, away from the ocean into a corner of the course flanked by luxurious homes. Hope struck a fine drive and then faded a 3-wood shot.

"There was a little wind in my kisser," he recalls, "and a tree in my line of flight to the green. Demaret came over to check my club. I never saw him that way before. He was always cute and joking, but here was Mr. Demaret, a pro at work. The way he looked at me I thought he was the house detective."

Demaret asked, "What have you got in your hand?"

Hope pointed to the 4-wood.

"He just grabbed that club away from me," Hope says, "and gave me a brassie. Then he growled, 'Hit it as hard as you can.' "

There was a five-minute delay while the way was cleared. Demaret glanced at the tree 75 yards ahead of the ball, and got another idea. He would give Hope a new grip for the shot.

"Bob hooked every wood he ever hit," Demaret said later. "He had to slice one around that tree. I set his left hand on the club and told him, 'Hit it out to the left. It'll bend around the tree if you do it my way.' "

Hope hit the shot flush, rolling it up onto the green. "Jimmy Thomson, the long-ball hitter, was in our foursome," Hope says. "He was on the green by the time I got there and he said, 'Buddy, just take your time.' The ball wasn't six inches from the hole. With my handicap stroke it was a net eagle three."

Hope knew almost everyone at Pebble Beach—pros, celebrities, low-handicap amateurs, society people from San Francisco, high rollers up from Palm Desert, bartenders, caddies, the locker room attendants. He treated them all with the same casual warmth, but his favorite was Demaret, whom he respected not only as a great player but also as a comedian of considerable skill.

Paired with Jimmy in the first round at Cypress Point in 1953, Hope hit a terrible drive off the first tee, duck-hooking the ball into an unplayable lie. "Don't worry, Bob," Demaret smiled. "There's always next year."

Hope could serve as Demaret's straight man. "Can I get home from here?" Bob asked his partner on the 13th fairway at Pebble Beach. "I dunno," replied Demaret. "Where do you live?"

After Hope and Demaret had stood the night watch at one of Francis Brown's parties, Hope greeted his pale, shaken partner the next morning at Cypress Point. Breaking into a little tune from *My Fair Lady,* Hope stared at Demaret and crooned,

> "I've grown accustomed to your face,
> *Although the parts are out of place."*

It was Hope who once termed Pebble Beach "Alcatraz with grass." Teamed with Mike Souchak in 1957, he blooped his tee shot into the trees on the first hole at Pebble Beach. The ball struck a limb and caromed back into the middle of the fairway. "That," he announced to Souchak, "is a bank shot, my boy. Shall we raise the ante to $50 a hole?"

Hope was forever on stage, ready with a quip. Art Rosenbaum remembers the time in 1953 when Les Keiter was doing network radio coverage of the tournament near the 18th green of the Monterey Peninsula Country Club. Keiter asked Rosenbaum to provide a brief rundown of the scores. Hope happened to stroll by at that moment and Keiter stuck the microphone in his face.

"Bob, a word please," Keiter said. It was too much for Hope to resist.

"I hooked one shot so badly today the 'tilt' sign went up on a tree," he began. "On behalf of Crosby—and who wouldn't want to be half of Crosby with the loot that guy has—I'd like to say this is the place for the elite, where ocean and golf ball meet." Then he was gone.

Hope and Crosby became American institutions over thirty years ago when they appeared together in the *Road* movies and each had his own radio show on NBC. There have been rumors in recent years that their public needling of each other contained some real darts, that their friendship had deteriorated. Hope is eager to dispel them, and of course that leads to another story.

"I don't see too much of Bing anymore, since he moved up north to Hillsborough," Hope says. "But I love the guy, and always will. We finally got a chance a few years ago to spend some time together again. We

went over to England to film *Road to Hong Kong* and lived on location in the same house. We ran over to Sunningdale and Wentworth to play golf after work. I was in this scene where a girl was painting my toes in a harem. Later we rushed over to the golf course and I was sitting there barefooted in the locker room. This English fellow comes in, takes one look at my toenails, and you know what he was thinking.

"The next day we did a scene where we came back from the moon and they were throwing confetti all day. I went right out and played golf again, and when I was getting ready to shower, I took off my shorts in front of two Scotsmen, and all the confetti fell out. They thought I hadn't taken a bath since New Year's."

Hope's fondest memories of Bing are of their days together at Lakeside Golf Club in Los Angeles, back in the late 1930s and early 1940s. "Bing was one of the original crowd," he says. "What a place that was. They had every movie star. W. C. Fields

. . . Edgar Kennedy . . . Babe Hardy . . . Stan Laurel . . . Leon Errol. You'd see Howard Hughes there with Jean Harlow."

After years of playing golf together for the Victory Caravan and World War II bond drives, Hope and Crosby continued as a fairway pair in tournaments like the one George May sponsored at Tam O'Shanter in Chicago. "One day 28,000 people showed up to watch us," Hope recalls. "I don't think many of them had ever been on a golf course before. They'd come to a ball in the fairway and stand around in a circle. We'd have to say, 'Open up, please. We go *that* way.'

"Playing golf with Bing was a riot. He swings so slowly that guys would pick his club out of his arms and check the trade name during his backswing."

Hope always claimed that Bing, despite their friendship, never gave him a preferential starting time in the Crosby. "One year," Bob says, "I teed off so early at Cypress that a deer on the first fairway fed me a gag line."

Tal Josselyn wrote an affectionate tribute to Hope in the Monterey Peninsula *Herald*. It read:

He stands there over the ball, bareheaded and gum-chewing, with his feet pointed at 11 and 1 o'clock. Then he starts down the fairway with his minstrel-show strut-stride. A genuinely good guy, making his shots and making his wisecracks. Who could ever forget him?

Nobody enjoyed the Crosby more than Bob Hope. Whether he was gagging, as with Phil Harris on opposite page, or competing earnestly, Hope always entertained the galleries.

The Weather: A Stormy Backdrop

No sporting event anywhere has been more closely associated with the weather than the Crosby. Writers have been writing about it and golfers complaining about it for nearly forty years. As Bing once observed, "There's lots of it."

"Bing's tournament," remarked Bob Hope, "is a real test of endurance. You expect wind and rain, and usually get it. But one day there were clams in the rain."

One of Los Angeles *Times* columnist Jim Murray's greatest delights is watching the pros struggle with the elements at Monterey. On a January day in 1965 he wrote:

If Bob Hope and Bing Crosby ever want to get together to do a picture on the Crosby golf tournament, I got the title for them—"The Road to Pneumonia." The "Chilblain Open," they ought to call it. The "Penicillin Open." The Smith Bros. ought to sponsor it. You need 14 clubs and a mustard plaster. Seven thousand guys fight to get an invitation to an oxygen tent and a fever chart. They can get the same sensation by standing in a bucket of ice, turning on a 10,000-horsepower fan in their faces and hiring someone to spray them with a fire hose and shoot sand in their eyes.

You see celebrities like Andy Williams and Jim Garner standing around the scoreboard praying they will make the cut and be able to go out one more day in this Yukon of golf and buck for a sore throat. You are reminded of an Abe Lincoln story of the guy who was asked how he felt about being tarred and feathered and ridden out of town on a rail and replied, 'If it weren't for the honor of the thing, I'd rather walk.'"

In conditions Bing described as "appearing with annoying frequency" a lonely golfer and caddie seek momentary sanctuary from a January squall.

In another weather-related column on the Crosby, Murray wrote:

Of all the tournaments, I guess my favorite is the Crosby. I guess it's because I enjoy watching people get shock treatment. The trouble with the pros is that they don't know how tough this game is. They usually tee up in nice sunny weather with a slight breeze at their backs, the fairways hard, the greens medium fast and the crowd quiet and respectful. The Crosby is something else. That's the tournament where they find out what a chamber of horrors 18 holes of golf can be. The clouds scud in low and gray. The wind turns your ears purple. The cold makes your nose run and your eyes watery. The rain makes a swamp of the fairway. The pros hate it. Know why? Because they have to play the game the way you and I play it.

I have to think it's good for them. Into each life, a little Crosby must fall. Caruso had to sing occasionally with off-key orchestras. Or lousy acoustics. Michaelangelo probably didn't always have the finest of pigments. Pavlova might have had to dance a time or two in borrowed shoes that were too tight. Bernhardt might have had to play some death scenes in a shower of ripe tomatoes in hick towns.

The 1952 Crosby was that kind of a character builder. The opening round was played in an all-day deluge and bone-chilling winds measured up to sixty-two miles per hour. "There was no casual water," recalls Cary Middlecoff, "because it had all frozen. Slabs of ice were blowing down the fairways."

By the time he reached the 16th hole at Cypress Point, Middlecoff had suffered enough. He and the other members of his foursome marked their balls on the green with tees and headed back to the sanctuary of the locker room at Pebble Beach.

Encountering the towering figure of Peter Hay, the Pebble Beach pro, Middlecoff explained his defection. "The wind was blowing so hard, Peter," he said, "the ball wouldn't stay up on the tee."

Hay, a Scottish-born traditionalist, snorted in anger. "Show me in the Rules of Golf," he brayed, "where ya have to tee the ball. Now get back out there and play."

Under today's more stringent tournament regulations any golfer walking in before play was officially halted would be disqualified. Things were more informal in those days.

Middlecoff returned to the 16th green to hole out, and as he stood over the putt, a strange sight caught his eye. "It was Grant Withers, the big Western actor," he said. "The wind had whipped up inside the pockets of his rainsuit and torn it off him. Withers was holding onto a cypress tree for dear life."

The 16th and 17th holes at Cypress Point, exposed to the full velocity of the ocean winds, are always the most hazardous spots in bad weather. Guy Wolstenholme, a British pro, walked into a patch of ice plant one year to retrieve an errant shot, fell down and broke his elbow. Less than an hour later, a San Francisco spectator named Lawrence Lucchesi got his feet caught in the ice plant during heavy winds and tumbled twenty feet to the rocks below, breaking his shoulder. One of Lucchesi's friends, unaware how badly he was hurt, shouted down to him, "What do you lie?"

The 17th measures 375 yards from the back tees. Under normal conditions it requires no more than an 8-iron approach, but the wind was blowing in off the ocean with such ferocity in that opening round of 1952 that Jimmy Demaret needed a driver, brassie and a hard 4-iron to reach the green.

"Jimmy one-putted for his par," smiled Bob Hope, his amateur partner. "He lit up like a Christmas tree whenever the wind blew. I think he was born in a gale down in Texas. His mother had to run five miles to retrieve him."

Demaret shot 74 that day, a remarkable score under those conditions, and then accompanied Hope and Crosby over to Fort Ord, where Bing did his radio show. There was a call there for Bing from Maurie Luxford, the harassed tournament director.

"Mangrum and Middlecoff have walked in," Luxford said. "They want to know when you're going to call it. Bing, it's getting pretty bad."

Demaret grabbed the phone away from Crosby. "Come on, Maurie, make 'em play," he said. "If I can finish, so can they."

The first round was not called off, but the second round was, and Demaret shot 71 on the final day to win the 36-hole tournament with a 145.

Four years later actor Randolph Scott was playing the 16th at Cypress, paired with Doug Ford. Against a forty-mile-an-hour wind, Ford hit a sizzling 2-iron shot. The ball looked as though it would carry to the flagstick, but the headwinds curled it back and it fell short of the cliff.

"Play your driver, Randy," Ford advised, "and lay it up over the short cut."

Scott hit his drive over the narrowest inlet, and pitched on. Before he could mark his ball, another gale came up and blew it off the green. Sam Snead, walking down 17, broke up in hysterical laughter. "You can chase it, Randy," he shouted, "but you'll never catch it."

Scott chipped the ball back onto the green and then, down on his knees to brace himself against the wind, holed the putt for a bogey 4. "With my stroke," he said, "it gave me a three. It was the toughest par I've ever had."

Conditions were just as bad the next year when Scott was paired with Harry Weetman, a British pro. Scott figured he had himself a good horse for foul-weather golf. On the practice green, Weetman looked at the black sky, smiled conspiratorially and said, "I'm used to playing in this stuff. The wind and the rain make me feel I'm right back at old Troon. Grand place, that."

Teeing off at Cypress Point, Weetman wore only a thin blue sweater over a short-sleeved shirt. Scott, bundled as though he were on Russian maneuvers, couldn't understand it. "That man must be awful tough," Randy told his caddie. Off they went. By the third hole, Harry Weetman's lips had turned blue. He never finished the round.

Thirteen others picked up that year, including Byron Nelson and Gene Sarazen. Sarazen was playing in the Crosby for the first time since it moved to the Monterey Peninsula. The weather didn't surprise him as much as the remarkable durability of the galleries. "The weather I can understand," he said. "But the people—never."

The most memorable year of bad weather was 1962, when it snowed on Saturday night. It not only set the final round back to Monday, but it created enormous national publicity for the Monterey Peninsula—the kind it could do without.

That night Elliott Henry, the West Coast promotions director for ABC, went to dinner with Cliff Dektar, one of his publicity men. As they walked the block from their hotel to the restaurant, Henry sniffed the air. He had lived in Chicago for seventeen years before moving to California, and he recognized

A rainy-weather interview at Pebble Beach involving Bob Crosby, Phil Harris, Doug Sanders, Jim McKay and Ralph Kiner. Above, the symbol of the 33rd Crosby in 1974: the tournament program sinking in a bunker full of water.

—or at least thought he did—the tingle in the air.

"I think it's going to snow tonight," he said.

Dektar, a Los Angeles native, shook his head.

"Are you kidding? It hasn't snowed here in forty years."

"Maybe so, but I say it's going to snow."

People stared out of their windows the next morning to a blanket of white. Pebble Beach looked like the North Pole.

"I know I got loaded last night," mused Jimmy Demaret over a morning bloody mary. "But how did I wind up at Squaw Valley?"

There were times, too, when the weather wasn't so humorous, and the conditions became hazardous. On the 18th hole at Pebble Beach in the final round of 1966, Jack Nicklaus hooked his drive into the ocean. He drove again, and hit it just over the seawall, on the marshy cliff. As Nicklaus and PGA tournament official George Walsh were looking for the second ball, the ground gave way and Walsh tumbled into the ocean, just missing Jack's outstretched hand. "Bon voyage," laughed Nicklaus, before helping to retrieve him.

Walsh was also involved in another potentially serious water incident in 1967. Jerry Pittman was playing the 17th hole at Cypress Point when his second shot landed in the ice plant at the edge of a cliff. Walsh was called on the scene for a ruling.

Pittman decided to test the place where the ball had landed to see if he could swing the club, or take a penalty drop. Suddenly the ground gave way under his feet, and Pittman was about to fall sixty feet into a cluster of jagged boulders below the cliff. Walsh reached out and grabbed him by the arm, as the muddy chunks tumbled down to the rocks. "The people in the gallery," related the shaken Walsh, "thought Jerry was a goner."

Pittman, understandably, was a trifle shaken himself. Tied with Billy Casper for the lead at that point in the third round, he bogeyed the next two holes.

That was the year the tournament committee hired a weather forecaster, at $50 a day. His prediction for Saturday's play was "clear and sunny." It poured so hard the round was called off. The weatherman reported, from his office in downtown Monterey, that it was indeed "clear and sunny."

Nobody seems to remember that the weather has frequently been favorable for the Crosby. In 1972 Tony Jacklin came over to play in the tournament, packing long underwear, heavy woolen knickers, sweaters and raingear. The sun shone warmly through the entire week as Jacklin scratched and sweltered in his woolens.

For a sustained period of aggravation, however, nothing in Crosby history could compare to the 1974 tournament. It was held during the first week of January and the rains, which began falling shortly after Christmas, never abated.

The irony was that the tournament originally had been scheduled for the third week of February. Then the Monterey merchants remembered that those dates fell over Washington's Birthday, one of their biggest resort weekends of the year. The hotels were already overbooked. So the Crosby traded dates with the Los Angeles Open, which was then the traditional opener on the tour.

The Crosby golfers needed a kayak more than a caddie. Thursday's round was washed out, hail delayed play for nearly two hours on Saturday, and the Monday round was postponed until the tournament was called off at 4 P.M. and shortened to 54 holes.

Gary Player came in after his opening round on Friday and declared, "I couldn't find the rule for imbedded shoes." Bruce Fleisher claimed the only man who could have gotten around Spyglass was Mark Spitz with a butterfly stroke.

It took Tom Weiskopf nearly half an hour to thaw out in the press room before he could talk to the writers. "I couldn't believe how bad it was," he said. "I've got a good amateur partner, Johnny Swanson of San Francisco, and the only time I saw him for ten holes was on the tee. On the 10th fairway we huddled against the wind and looked for the group behind us. Nobody was there. They were smarter than we were; they had already quit."

Perhaps the most perceptive golfers were Phil Harris and Harry James. After a full evening at the Clambake the night before, they looked out their windows the next morning, crawled back into bed and withdrew.

"What we were playing out there," observed Nicklaus, "was certainly not golf. It's the first time I've ever been involved in a round where you could drop the ball closer to the hole," a concession made when there was no other suitable drop area available.

Claiming a sore back, Nicklaus withdrew a few hours before the tournament was officially terminated on Monday.

It reminded Jack Burke of a situation he had encountered over twenty years earlier, when he was paired on a stormy day at Cypress Point with George Coleman, Lawson Little and Francis H. I. Brown.

Standing under his umbrella on the first tee, Burke noticed that the wind had blown down the starter's stand. Turning to Little, Jack remarked, "I wonder why Bing doesn't call this thing off today."

Little, who had won a British Amateur in similar conditions, prided himself on his bad-weather golf. "That's the way it is with you young players," he told Burke. "A little weather rolls in and you want to run to the house."

By the third hole, Lawson Little's umbrella had blown inside out. But he was playing superbly, only 3 over par through 15 holes. On the 16th, into a fifty-mile-an-hour gale, Little adjusted his grip to hook the shot and keep it out of the ocean. After hitting four shots into the Pacific, Lawson looked at Jack Burke and said, "You would think Bing would call this damn thing off, wouldn't you?"

Tennessee Ernie Ford summed up the frustrations of bad-weather golf in the Crosby rather deftly. "I've worked all my life to keep from walking in the mud," he said. "But every year I pay $400 to come here and spend a week in it."

The Amateurs: Oscars for Supporting Roles

Sandwiched between the touring pros and the show business celebrities in the cast of characters at the Crosby are the 120 or so amateur players of varying credentials and handicaps ranging from scratch to 18. For thirty years the man who screened the 9,000 annual requests, before Bing made the final selections, was the late Maurie Luxford.

Until his death in 1971, Luxford served the Crosby as tournament director, starter, self-appointed buffer and general confidant to Bing and, above all, as godfather to the amateurs.

Maurie was a native of New Zealand who had served with the Anzacs in World War I, watching his closest friend die from shellfire in France two hours before the armistice. He migrated to the United States in 1919, became involved in various business and civic enterprises in Los Angeles and joined the Lakeside Golf Club in 1928.

Crosby and Luxford had adjacent lockers at Lakeside for years. They were pals from the day they met, and when Bing started his tournament in 1937 at Rancho Santa Fe, Maurie was there, as a competitor and official. He played well enough to win the pro-am with Johnny Revolta in 1939.

When the tournament moved north in 1947, Maurie assigned himself the dual tasks of starter and first tee announcer. "He loved that microphone," recalls Bob Hope. "You couldn't turn him off. He'd go on for three or four minutes with those elaborate introductions, reciting the player's lifetime accomplishments and, in my case, the titles of most of my movies."

One year at Pebble Beach, Johnny Weissmuller, the movie Tarzan, was late for his 7:15 A.M. tee-off. "Calling Johnny Weissmuller," Maurie boomed over the public address. "Last call for Johnny Weissmuller."

Awakened in his Del Monte Lodge room near the first tee, Don Cherry flung open the window in wrath and shouted, "Damn it, Luxford, look up in the tree."

Luxford was besieged by golfers wanting to play in the Crosby. One day, as Maurie was washing his hands in the men's room of the Los Angeles airport, a stranger approached him. "I've got $25,000 in my pocket," the man said. "It's yours if you get me into the Crosby."

He was serious and Luxford stared at him, then said, "I'm sorry, we don't operate that way."

There was a strong strain of sentiment in Luxford, however, for the amateur with a legitimate request. In 1969 he received a letter from an employee of the Citizens National Bank of Salinas, California, one Robin Harner. It said Harner was a high school dropout who had once caddied at Pebble Beach and Cypress Point.

"I've carried bags in several Crosby tournaments," Harner wrote, "and it's been my ambition someday to play in one."

Luxford forwarded the letter to Bing with a short note suggesting Harner's admission, and on December 16, 1969, Robin Harner received a reply. It read simply, "You're invited." It was signed by Bing Crosby.

Luxford's devotion to the amateurs is perpetuated by a trophy in his name, awarded annually by the 3M Company to the amateur who helps his pro the most.

Among the recipients has been Ed Crowley, an executive with The Sheraton

Maurie Luxford, attired in fiesta finery, directs traffic from the first tee at Pebble Beach. Luxford was the Crosby starter, announcer and tournament chairman for nearly 30 years.

Corp. who twice won the pro-am with Cary Middlecoff. Crowley played in twenty-six consecutive Crosby tournaments until 1975 when he decided, at the age of sixty-nine, he'd prefer just to kibitz and mix drinks for the boys.

Crowley always seemed to be in the middle of the action at the Crosby. He was hitting his drive on the 18th at Pebble Beach in the final round of play in 1951 at the moment Phil Harris holed his long birdie putt on 17 to clinch the pro-am with Dutch Harrison. "I was in the middle of my backswing when the ball rolled in," Crowley recalled. "The roar of the crowd sounded like the guns of Fort Ord."

Ed was Middlecoff's partner in 1956, the year Cary shot his memorable last-round 68 in a brutal storm to win the tournament. Middlecoff had recruited a man to carry his umbrella that day, a fellow who had been named college football's Coach of the Year two weeks earlier. Nobody in the gallery recognized Bud Wilkinson under his raincoat and poncho.

"That was the year we were walking along the second fairway with the rain pelting down and the wind howling," Crowley says. "I saw a guy go into one of those portable outhouses. A big gust of wind blew it over . . . while the guy was still in there."

In 1965 Crowley was waiting on the 7th tee at Pebble Beach when Eddie Merrins holed his tee shot into a blustery gale. "Eddie walked past me, holding the club like a scepter," Crowley recalls. "He said, 'Don't tell anyone what I used on that shot.' It was a 3-iron, on a 110-yard hole."

Crowley used to share a Del Monte Lodge suite along the 18th fairway with Middlecoff, Broadway star John Raitt and Raitt's wife, Marge. Raitt put himself in charge of cleaning the clubs and shining the shoes each night.

"We always took our clubs out of the car and brought them in for John," Crowley says. "One time we forgot. I had a late morning tee time at Pebble with Andy Williams, and when Marge Raitt asked to take the car over to Spyglass, we told her to go ahead. Then we remembered that the car was gone with our clubs, and it was time to get ready.

"We dashed over to Spyglass, looking for the car. Andy was getting desperate, and so was I. Finally we found it. We got a crowbar and banged and slashed away at the trunk of that brand new Buick. There was a big crowd around us.

"Finally here comes Marge Raitt, holding a set of keys in her hand. 'You boys weren't looking for these, were you?' she asked. We got back to Pebble just in time to tee off with our group."

As the years went by, Ed Crowley's Crosby routine seldom varied. Regardless of how late he'd been out the night before, he would rise at 6:30 in the morning, pull on his thermal underwear, tape his bifocals to his ears to keep the wind from blowing them off, and head for the muddy practice tee before spending up to 6 1/2 hours on the course.

One day Ed got the last bag of balls at the driving range. Don Cherry and Tommy Bolt, neither one distinguished by an even temperament, asked him for a few balls. "Okay," Crowley said, "but I've got a better idea. Why don't you guys just warm up by throwing a few clubs at each other?"

Another familiar amateur was Roger Kelly, a Los Angeles lawyer who was good enough to win the California Amateur. In his

Two classic examples of the diligent amateur spirit at the Crosby. Ed Crowley (above left) leans into a wood shot during his 25th straight appearance. Below, 3M Company president Ray Herzog battles rainy weather and Cypress Point rough.

In a festive night at Del Monte Lodge, San Francisco amateur Johnny Swanson commemorates Jack Nicklaus' twenty-second birthday with Alaska crab. Looking on: a happy Barbara Nicklaus.

younger days Kelly was a prodigious drinker, a handicap that seldom affected his golf. He belonged to Lakeside, and the story goes that people came from miles around to watch him hit a 1-iron or empty a bottle.

In 1947, Kelly had stayed up all night partying before the first round. Hurrying to join his pro partner, Sam Snead, on the first tee at Pebble Beach, Roger forgot to wear shoes. Feeling the need to regurgitate some whiskey, he headed into the bushes near the tee. Snead heard the groans of anguish and recognized the symptoms, but couldn't muster much sympathy. After all, the pro-am money was at stake and Sam hadn't come all the way to California for social golf.

Snead turned to Maurie Luxford and complained, "You paired me with this guy? He can't even stand up."

Kelly staggered over to Sam, and fixed a rheumy stare on him. "We're not only going to win the pro-am," he said thickly, "but here's $100 I beat you even-up." Sam declined the challenge, but they did win the pro-am and Kelly helped him 20 strokes for the 54 holes.

Roger Kelly went on to play in every Crosby for the next twenty-five years and ultimately took the pledge of sobriety.

Few Crosby amateurs have attained the competitive reputation of Johnny Swanson, a balding former San Francisco University halfback who runs a bowling alley in Daly City and plays to a rock-hard six at the Olympic Club. Swanson is a man not easily impressed by a celebrity.

A few years ago he was in Washington, D.C., and attended a White House dinner. Seated next to a governor, he engaged the politician at length in a discussion of world affairs. The governor assumed he was in the company of a leading industrialist or a governmental figure of significant stature. He asked Swanson what his line of work was.

"I run a bowling alley," Swanson replied. The governor suddenly involved himself in his demitasse.

Swanson met Crosby in 1936, when Bing's alma mater, Gonzaga, came down to play San Francisco U. Bing congratulated him after the game on his performance, and the bonds of an improbable friendship were initiated.

Swanson first met Jack Nicklaus in 1961, when Jack played Olympic as a tune-up before going down to Pebble Beach, where he was to win the U. S. Amateur. Swanson claims he had never heard of him. "How many strokes do I have to give you?" asked Nicklaus on the first tee. "Look, kid," countered the fat man, "who did you ever beat for money? I'll play you even-up."

Swanson was 3-up at the turn and the match finished even. They established a tradition of Wednesday practice rounds at Pebble Beach, Nicklaus and Bob Hoag against Swanson and pro Tom Weiskopf.

When Nicklaus celebrated his twenty-second birthday in the 1962 Crosby, Swanson treated Jack and Barbara to a dinner of Alaska king crab in the Del Monte Lodge. Midway through the meal, Swanson called Nicklaus over to the lobby phone with the explanation, "There's someone who wants to talk to you."

As Jack picked up the phone, he was greeted by the full rendition of "Happy Birthday to You." Puzzled and a little irritated, Nicklaus waited through it all and then inquired icily, "To whom am I speaking?"

"This is Bing Crosby."

"Oh, I'm sorry, I didn't recognize the voice."

In trouble. Almost engulfed by the rugged cliff-top landscape at Pebble Beach, a resolute golfer plays his shot

back to the 8th fairway. It could have been worse—on the beach or in the ocean.

Swanson's friend John Brodie holds the distinction of being the consistently best amateur to play in the Crosby. Brodie, the former quarterback with Stanford and the San Francisco 49ers, was so good at golf he turned pro for a while, but he discovered amateur golf was more fun and just about as lucrative. The Crosby and the Super Bowl frequently fell during the same week, and the standing gag was that the 49ers would never make it to the Super Bowl as long as Brodie kept getting invited to the Crosby.

In 1971 the 49ers were only one game away, but lost to Dallas for the National Conference championship. "I wanted the 49ers to win," said Bob Rosburg, another Stanford alumnus who was Brodie's partner in the Crosby, "but I was happy to have John back as a partner again. The year before he played better golf than either pro in the foursome."

Nobody could level that accusation against anyone who stayed in the Snake Pit, a suite in the annex of the Del Monte Lodge which serves annually as headquarters for a group of high-rolling amateurs from Southern California and Arizona.

The late Milt Hicks, a land baron from Palm Springs, was a charter member. When Hicks died, the Snake Pit tradition of around-the-clock living at the Crosby was perpetuated by Bill Worthing, Bob Goldwater, Dr. Phil Smith, Eddie Susalla and Joe Dyer.

Phil Harris didn't stay there officially, but could usually be located in front of the fireplace telling a story. Harris was the custodian of the Snake Pit's Calcutta credentials in the days when that event at the Monterey Peninsula Country Club, auctioneered by Bob Goldwater, provided a greater cash turnover than the pro purse.

Six Snake Pit regulars one year pooled their resources on select choices in the Calcutta. Every pro and team they purchased paid off, for sums totaling several thousands of dollars. But when it came time to collect, they came up empty. Harris had lost the stubs.

Ray Bolger, the entertainer who carries a 14-handicap at Bel-Air, was a Snake Pit regular. "You had to decide beforehand if you were going to be a golfer or a socializer," Bolger says. "You couldn't burn it at both ends with that gang, not playing those courses. Many's the time a man heard his name being announced at the first tee while he was still working on a last shot for the road."

Mickey Mantle, hobbling on an infected foot, once came into the Snake Pit for a bracer or two after a practice round and asked Bill Worthing to find a penknife and slit his ailing toenail. With Don Drysdale holding Mantle down, Worthing carved briefly and then decided to apply a heated needle to burn the toenail away. Unable to hold the hot needle, Worthing dropped it between Mantle's toes.

The Mick fled in terror, never to be seen in the Snake Pit again.

In recent years one of the most prominent amateurs at the Crosby has been Mickey Van Gerbig, a Palm Beach socialite the pros call "Sudden Summer" because of his rich tan. A scratch handicapper, Van Gerbig shot a natural 67 a couple of years ago at Pebble Beach while his pro partner, Deane Beman, was struggling to a 79.

Nelson Cullenward has done double duty at the Crosby for nearly three decades as a participant and golf writer for the San Francisco *Examiner*. A strong left-handed player, he has not appeared in every Crosby, but goes back to the days at

George Coleman and Jack Burke discuss their pro-am strategy in the top photo. Below, Governor Wendell Anderson of Minnesota looks right at home in the grim weather with stocking cap and ski jacket.

Rancho. In 1965 he and George Archer tied for first in the pro-am.

Bob Roos and Ed Lowery of San Francisco are both twenty-five-year Crosby veterans, Roos serving in recent years as an assistant to Bing in selecting the amateur field.

Although the Crosby entry fee for the amateurs is just $400, compared to $1,500 for the Hope, the expense of traveling and spending a week at Pebble Beach can be substantial. Jack Adams of Minneapolis, who built his own golf course, Olympic Hills, received a Crosby invitation in 1968. Minnesota winters precluding much preparation for tournament golf, Adams flew out to Palm Springs two weeks before the Crosby to sharpen his game. By the time he returned home, the project had cost him over $2,000.

In a class by himself is Lyle Guslander, a senior executive and major stockholder with a Hawaiian hotel and real estate firm. Guslander has an 18 handicap, the maximum allowed for the Crosby. He was invited to play in the 1975 tournament, and six weeks before the Crosby flew from his home island of Kaui to Honolulu, caught a jet to San Francisco and then took a short flight down to Monterey. He hurried out to Pebble Beach to play a practice round—and returned home the next day.

"I just thought if I was going to play in Bing's tournament," he said, "the least I could do was get a quick look at the golf course first."

Society: First-nighters on Display

It was inevitable that the Crosby would evolve into a social event. From the outset it had the right chemistry—show business personalities, top athletes and an elite list of amateur invitees. When the tournament moved to the Monterey Peninsula, it acquired the perfect setting.

Located conveniently to San Francisco, Los Angeles and Palm Springs, the peninsula has long been a mecca for society. Samuel F. B. Morse gave it that aura from the start. He moved in circles of the very rich and cultivated his little kingdom as a haven for the wealthy and beautiful people who quickly discovered the virtues of the Del Monte Forest.

There are approximately 1,800 homes in the forest, most of them in the six-figure bracket. A modest lot sells for about $40,000. For fifty-one weeks of the year the residents live in tranquil privacy, hedges shielding their comfortable homes from the gawking tourists who pay $3 per car to wind through the seventeen-mile drive.

Then hordes of outsiders pour in for the Crosby, clogging the four gates of the forest—Carmel, Hill, Lighthouse and Country Club. The regulars regard the intrusion with a grudging tolerance, but the Crosby is nevertheless as fully a social occasion as a competitive tournament. At night the lights glitter brightly in the rambling homes. Sophisticated conversation and the tinkle of ice echo through the woods.

Charles Denton has observed in the San Francisco *Examiner:*

They come in droves—a mixture of society and sweat sox that's probably unique in the trade, even though tournament golf has become as much a social as an athletic pursuit. Everybody who is anybody and has spiked shoes is here. But their privacy gets a certain amount of protection from the fact that everybody who isn't anybody and has spiked shoes is here, too.

Guys who couldn't break 100 shooting at a hole in the living room carpet stand in front of the official scoreboard making knowing remarks about how Jack's game is off today and Arnie can't straighten out his drives.

For the permanent citizenry, the Crosby seems to be the highlight of the social season. A French election doesn't have as many parties. It's also the height of the socialism season, inasmuch as the householder who doesn't string barbed wire across his driveway is liable to find that he's landlord to a house-trailer the next morning.

It's to their credit that they take this invasion with surprisingly good nature, especially when you consider that unless they're awfully lucky, the fairway residents are very apt to have their lawns stomped into something that looks like an alligator farm.

Frances Moffat, former society editor of the San Francisco *Chronicle*, caught the spirit of Crosby Week with this account in a 1966 column:

There are three worlds at the Cypress Point Club, which was the place to be yesterday on opening day of the Crosby tournament.

One is the already large gallery of golf and celebrity fans who mill around the caddie house or circle the first tee. The women wear stretch pants and ask players like Dean Martin and Phil Harris for

Kathy Crosby (left) chats in the Del Monte Lodge
with Aime Michaud, former president of Del Monte
Properties, and Mrs. Milton Coburn, the widow of
Samuel F. B. Morse.

Francis H. I. Brown and Winona Love, the genial
hosts for many a Crosby shindig. Brown was a
superb golfer in his younger days and continued to
play tournament golf well into his seventies.

autographs. They drink highballs in paper cups and when the big names are gone they go off to the next scene of action.

Another group at Cypress is composed of members of the exclusive golf club, the only people who are admitted to the clubhouse—although many try to get in during the tournament. They arrive in limousines or imported sports cars, and the women wear sensible tweeds and camel hair coats. The reward for membership is a chance to chat with each other about the tournament and enjoy cocktails and lunch in the privacy of the white Colonial style clubhouse.

The inner circle at Cypress is even smaller than this group. It is made up of the four couples who are actually staying at the clubhouse during the tournament. In residence this year are the Bing Crosbys, the William Boyds, the James B. Blacks, Jr. and the John L. Bradleys.

A decade later, society coverage of the Crosby had changed little. The same people are still partying in the same lovely homes, for the most part. Newspapers from the Bay Area and the peninsula devote many columns of space to the glittering socialites, informing the readers where they partied, what they drank and what they served for buffet dinners.

Reported the San Francisco *Chronicle:*

Unquestionably it was beautiful in the weather and people department down at Pebble Beach for the 34th Crosby Pro-Am. The local crew threw out the welcome mat on Monday when many people arrived to stay at various homes in Pebble Beach. House parties have become a way of the good life at the Crosby.

Again, Francis Brown and Winona Love had a full house which included George

and Clarissa Dyer, the Kenneth Browns (he's Francis' nephew from Honolulu) and Mary Henderson from England, and each night they added even more people for dinner parties. Winona said, 'We have a small house so we've only been having little dinners for 30.'

Among Thursday night's 30 were the Jack Lemmons, the Clint Eastwoods and [Tennessee] Ernie Ford. Then on Friday, guests included Stuyvie Fish and Sandy Waters. Dawn Coleman of Palm Beach showed up at dinner Friday without husband George, because he never goes out at night when he's playing in the tournament. The Bing Crosbys also dropped by for drinks before dinner.

The San Jose *Mercury* devoted an entire page to society coverage, leading off with this tidbit:

Whether on or off the fairways at Pebble Beach, the Crosby Clambake has been fun, fun, fun! . . . the spectators came in droves to see their favorite celebrities such as George C. Scott, Ephrem Zimbalist, Jr., Jack Lemmon and Bob Stack, among others, paired with the top playing pros . . . At sundown the parties begin.

In the Oakland *Tribune:*

There were parties aplenty at the 34th annual Bing Crosby golf tournament, concluding yesterday with the elegant brunch given by Del Monte Properties president Alfred Gawthrop in the terrace room at Del Monte Lodge . . . it featured such delicacies as crab, shrimp, crayfish, roast prime rib of beef, pecan pie, champagne and chocolate eclairs. . . .

Merv Griffin, who bought a house at Pebble a few years ago, gave his own Crosby party Friday night. Clint and Maggie

And The Beat Goes On At The Crosby

Mr. and Mrs. George Coleman entertained for their Monterey Peninsula friends Tuesday night at a dinner and dancing party in a private dining room at Del Monte Lodge.

The Colemans are here from Palm Beach, Fla., on their annual visit while Mr. Coleman plays in The Crosby.

The Steins' Crosby Party

Dr. and Mrs. Jack Stein gave a "Crosby party" for between 70 and 80 guests Thursday at their Carmel home. Their guests included Mr. and Mrs. Clayton Russell of Piedmont and Mrs. Edmund McCarthy of Orinda, who are visiting the Steins during the tournament.

Also among their guests were John Lotz, one of the players, and Mrs. Lotz of Hayward; many friends from The Beach and Tennis Club, including the Ray Marches; and Peter Paxton, who is masterminding the new Carmel Valley Racquet Club, now in its planning stages and to be situated near the Carmel Valley Golf and Country Club.

The Heids Were Hosts

Mr and Mrs Alexander Heid Jr., of Scarsdale, N.Y. and Pebble Beach, have as houseguests in their Padre lane home, during the Crosby tournament, Mr. and Mrs. Jack Munger of Dallas (he is playing in the tournament) and the S. Champion Tituses of Hillsborough.

The Heids entertained for their guests at a cocktail buffet for 60 Wednesday evening at The Beach and Tennis Club.

Frank Fees Entertained

Mr. and Mrs. Frank Fee were hosts at a cocktail buffet Wednesday evening at their Monterey Peninsula Country Club home, entertaining in honor of out-

Society Calls

BY MARY LOU LOPER
Times Staff Writer

It's not all golf in Bing's 27th Am.

There's some whistling, people-watching, some wal some partying, some church-g some weather.

But through it all, you ha keep in mind the tournament gram's sage advice: "Remem golf ball is made of hard rubb can travel 153 miles per hour. could crack a coconut. Give th ers plenty of room."

Two Sunday Parties

The Bay Area and Monterey Peninsula newspapers give the Crosby almost as much space on the society pages as they do in the sports section. Many names wind up in both.

Happy Crosby Party

A happy event during the early part of Crosby Week was the cocktail buffet party given at the Monterey Peninsula Country Club home of Cmdr. (USN ret) and

Weekend Windup

Of the Clambake

Crosby Clambake Inspires
A Round of Entertaining

Reise
J.

A full and interesting week is ahead for those who plan to attend Bing Crosby's great golf tournament at Pebble Beach Thursday through Sunday. Many house parties have been planned and numerous other parties will honor those who will be at Pebble Beach for the tournament.

Visiting Mr. and Mrs. Samuel

Mr. and Mrs. William Clay Ford of Detroit, Dennis O'Keefe, John Hodiak, Mr. and Mrs. Johnny Weismuller, Dennis Morgan, and John de Blois Wack of Santa Barbara.

Mrs. William May Garland of Los Angeles will open her Pebble Beach home for the event, bringing her son and daughter-in-law

Socialites Throng Pebble Beach

TALES OUT OF MAYFAIR

By FRANCES MOFFAT
Society Editor, The Examiner

PEBBLE BEACH, Jan. 16. —THE BING CROSBY tournament is living up to its reputation for sport thrills and party fun, despite the weather, which has been generally

there, forcing them to give their cocktail parties and dress for the evening's festivities by flashlight and candles.

CONSIDERING yesterday's weather, it's amazing so many turned out to watch the players on the courses at Cypress Point and the Monterey Country Club. Spectators could scarcely be described as fashionably attired. Anything went, including a leopard jacket combined with matador trousers and a parka.

and Fred Whitman looked like characters from outer space in the waterproof nylon trousers and tops in which they played on the Pebble Beach course while it was free of tournament contestants. The two were down for the weekend with the Stuart Heatleys. The latter's interest concentrated on the Cypress Point Club, where Mr. Heatley competed in the match.

The fairways at Cypress were as popular as they were fashionable, with many luncheon

their cottage at the lodge, where Tom later joined her in greeting a succession of guests.

The Heatleys, Vivienne Raven and Fred Whitman stopped off before returning to Carmel, and the Patrick Peabodys of Los Gatos came by with the Stewart Moores of Oakland and Thomas White of San Francisco, who were with them at their Rio Del Mar beach place. Later, Dr. and Mrs. Albert Rowe Jr. of Piedmont arrived with an account of a rough

Gene Littler and Bud Holscher, and their wives.

Miss Winona Love, wearing a short black lace gown, was hostess at the party. The patio, filled with many rare island plants, was canvassed over and there was dancing to Red Nickels' orchestra.

The young set partied last night as guests of the Harry C. Hunts Jr., at the home of his parents, the senior Hunts in Pebble Beach. This group included the house party of the Peter Hatelys, Sarah Coleman and her houseguests, Sarahbelle Dibble and Joe Cebrian Pringle; Patsy and Dan Walcott Jr., Dolly Fritz, Barbara Register, Phil Stevenson and Gordon Johnson.

On Friday night, the Robert

Stanton's were hosts at cocktails, while Tom Bunn entertained still others at a similar function.

NOTEBOOK JOTTINGS ... Mrs. Carl Livingston and the Henry N. Kuechlers Jr. dropping in at the lodge ... They were among the weekend guests at the Fred Scribners' home in Pebble Beach ... Betty and Gordon Dennis enjoying the tournament during their annual winter vacation in Monterey ... Mr. and Mrs. Jake Butts, who annually come out from Wichita, Kans., for the tournament, celebrating the purchase of a new home in Pebble Beach ... Both are Stanfordites and have many friends in the Bay area.

Mrs. Charles de Limur and Mrs.

in Crosby Pro-Am

CHRISTY FOX

How Did They Find Time
for Golf at Pebble Beach?

PEBBLE BEACH: The afterglow of the Crosby Clambake is a melange of

and Ray Herzog (who is prexy of 3-M, one of the Clambake's sponsors) ,

try Club with a view of the ocean, silhouetted cypress trees and even a

Final Festive Touch to Crosby Tournament

Eastwood were there, and so was beautiful Rosemarie Stack, the members of Merv's TV band and singer Glen Campbell, who joined his host in song during the evening.

In the Monterey Peninsula *Herald:*

Kathryn Crosby has done right well in making the scene sparkle with her presence, in spite of her TV commitments. Hank and Rolande Ketcham [creator of Dennis the Menace] left Dania, their little one, home in Geneva, Switzerland, because they felt there were too many time zones for her to cope with between Geneva and Pebble Beach, but they'll be hurrying home after the Crosby for her second birthday on February 1.

The cartoonist, who now lives in Geneva, has been on the Crosby scene for twenty-two years. He and his striking Austrian wife are high on the guest list for the most exclusive parties, along with the Clint Eastwoods, the Bob Stacks, Phil Harris and his wife, Alice Faye, and Bob and Dolores Hope.

Recently one of the most sought-after invitations is that to the annual Saturday night cocktail party in the Del Monte Lodge library hosted by Bing and Ray Herzog, president and chief executive officer of 3M. Herzog, a medium-handicapper from St. Paul, plays in the tournament, followed diligently in each round by several of his younger corporate executives.

Bing has always felt comfortable among the Del Monte people and their guests, particularly since his marriage to Kathy. They move smoothly through the society strata, perhaps having lunch one day with the Charles de Brettevilles of Pebble Beach, walking a few holes with actor Bob Sterling and his beautiful actress wife, Anne Jeffreys,

a cocktail or two at the Richard Dirickson home in Pebble Beach and frequently having dinner at Cypress Point with the George Colemans.

Without a doubt the most sociable socialite ever to appear on the Crosby scene was Francis H. I. Brown. The scion of a wealthy family in Hawaii, Brown used to laughingly admit he was born not only with a silver spoon in his mouth, but with several million dollars in his pocket.

Few men have ever derived more enjoyment from such good fortune.

He is well into his eighties now, the good times mostly behind him. But in his prime he was a magnificent golfer, good enough to win the Hawaiian, California and Japanese Amateur championships in the early 1930s. He shot 64 in a practice round at Pebble Beach and 66 at St. Andrews.

Francis had been an ambulance driver in World War I, a champion swimmer, a 10-goal polo player and, in the estimation of another reputable native of the Islands, Pebble Beach pro Art Bell, the longest hitter among amateur players of his day.

In 1935 Brown was riding in a car that struck a tree at high speed, demolishing the auto and killing another passenger. They thought Francis was dead, too. He was taken to the morgue, but managed to wiggle his toes as the sheet was about to be placed over him.

The accident crushed Brown's hips and fractured his pelvis in five places. His golf was never as good after that, but he was such a fixture at Pebble Beach that a special ruling allowed him to ride in a cart, often chauffered by George Coleman's wife, Dawn, while he continued to play in the Crosby.

Crosby's first exposure to Francis Brown

came when Bing was a young singer with Paul Whiteman's band. They played golf together occasionally, and when Bing launched his tournament, one of his first invitations went to Brown.

For the next thirty-five years, Francis was a regular at Bing's tournament, holding memorable parties either at his Del Monte Forest home or in one of the cottages he rented along the first fairway at Pebble Beach to handle the overflow.

Brown was equally proficient with a golf club or a cocktail glass in his hands.

"The guy is truly an incredible character," Bing says. "In 1930 he entered the U. S. Amateur at Merion, the one Bobby Jones won for his Grand Slam. Brown could really play. He brought a big group of boosters along with him to Philadelphia, including some high rollers from Hawaii. They put a lot of money on him to win the qualifying medal, and after the first round he was among the leaders.

"They threw a lot of cocktail parties in those nice homes along the Merion fairways, and on the back nine of his second round, when he still had a good chance to be the qualifying medalist, Francis stopped in for a few drinks. He never finished the round.

"A couple of years later he was playing over in Scotland, at Gleneagles, and scored a hole-in-one early in his round. He sent back instructions to the hotel bar that the drinks were on him until 5 o'clock. Well, you know those Scots. The word got around quickly, and they came in from all over to have a few toddies. Francis forgot to close the bar, and the next day he got the bill. It was over $6,000. Brownie paid it without batting an eye."

Jimmy Demaret remembers with particular fondness the daiquiris Brown has mixed for guests during the Crosby. "He made a special kind for Bob Hope," Demaret says. "Bob liked them so well that Francis wore out his mixer."

Inevitably there formed a firm friendship between Francis and another equally ardent patron of the sauce, Phil Harris. "I always felt the reason I never played as well as I would have liked in Bing's tournament was that Francis kept me up too late at night," Harris says. "He is the all-time host."

Brown was a dominant figure in the establishment of amateur and professional golf in Hawaii, financially aiding several pros and heading the Francis Brown Junior Golf Foundation.

"The story I've always liked about Francis," says Hal Wood, a Honolulu journalist, "is the one about the day he received a check for $6 million on the sale of some land at Pearl Harbor to the federal government. That night, while out on the town celebrating, he ran short of money and attempted to cash the check at a bar. The bartender looked at the check and fainted."

Ted Durein, press director of the Crosby ever since it moved to the Monterey Peninsula in 1947, once wrote in the tournament program that no man was ever pin high on the par-5 18th at Pebble Beach in 2. Brown took issue. "I was," he told Durein, and he had been, on the day he shot his 64.

During the awards ceremony of the 1961 Clambake, Bing presented Brown with a solid silver cup dating back to 1761 and proclaimed him as "the most beloved afficionado of the game."

Nobody who ever knew Francis Brown would dispute that claim.

TV: A Nation Views the Performance

If there ever was a golf tournament tailored for television, the Crosby is it. With its ineffable blend of scenic courses, pros and celebrities, dramatic seacoast weather and a captive winter audience in many parts of the country, the Crosby has become a January tradition in the living rooms of America.

It set an all-time golf telecast record by reaching 11,540,000 homes on a Sunday afternoon in 1971, immediately following the Super Bowl coverage, and was beamed into 10,070,000 homes on the Sunday round of 1975.

The Crosby ranked No. 1 among all golf tournaments in television ratings for 1972 and 1973, slipped to fourth in 1974 and took a commanding lead early on the 1975 tour, according to A. C. Nielsen figures.

The cost for commercial TV sponsorship in 1975 was approximately $40,000 for each minute, producing gross revenues of nearly $1 million for ABC. The bill for the 3M Company of Minnesota, which sponsored one-third of the telecast, was well over $300,000.

One of the primary reasons for the Crosby's enormous appeal, in the view of television people, is the prospect of watching a personality like Jack Lemmon taking three swipes at a ball buried in a bunker. The celebrities have long recognized the publicity value of television exposure in the Crosby, but that has to be measured against the chance of making an absolute fool of one's self in front of millions.

Nobody has experienced both to a more substantial degree or taken the ordeal more graciously than Jack Lemmon. Lemmon

Television's ubiquitous eye hovers over the 18th green at Pebble Beach, with the gallery and lodge in background. The Crosby has been telecast nationally since 1958.

is fifty years old and has spent the greater part of his adult life performing in front of audiences and cameras. But the prospect of hitting golf shots in a televised tournament terrifies him.

"I would rather play Hamlet with no rehearsal in an opera house than play golf on television," Lemmon admits. "On the stage or a movie set, I'm in control on familiar ground. On the golf course, I'm playing someone else's game."

Lemmon's first exposure to the cameras at Pebble Beach came on the 14th hole of the third round in 1959. Chopping and dubbing frightfully, he finally came within TV range. "And now here's Jack Lemmon, about to hit that all-important eighth shot," remarked Jim McKay from the tower behind the green.

After chunking a wedge, Lemmon skulled his chip shot from just off the green. The ball rolled uphill toward the hole and died, then began rolling back, gathering momentum until it trickled off the green and between Jack's legs. ABC replayed the sequence over and over.

"Jack's getting more footage here today," observed Bing, "than he has in his last three films."

Byron Nelson the ABC analyst, broke down Lemmon's swing in slow motion—and detected eleven major flaws.

The ABC people later edited the film of that shot, doctored it to speed up the sequence, and presented it to his wife, actress Felicia Farr. "She threw a birthday party for me," Jack recalls, "and played it about a dozen times for the guests."

Lemmon continued to botch up his round that day, as the cameras kept returning to him. "When we got to 17, the long par-3, we had a little wind behind us," he says. "I cranked up and hit a driver. It went forty

A grimace of anguish by Jack Lemmon after another flubbed shot. The veteran actor admits he is "petrified" by the prospect of playing golf in front of a TV camera.

yards over the green. 'That's the only good shot you've hit all day, Jack,' Jim Garner said. 'Unfortunately it's in the ocean.' "

Standing in the water and rocks, Lemmon swung a wedge and flailed the ball 130 yards farther out into the ocean.

On the 18th hole he knocked two tee shots out of bounds, reached the green in 9 and carefully surveyed his 35-foot putt. Asked which way it broke, Lemmon's caddie replied, "Who cares?"

Andy Williams endured a similar embarrassment in 1966, his first year in the Crosby. "On the 18th hole at Pebble Beach," Andy says, "I hit a low hard shot that bored into the side of a trap, against a wall of sand two feet high. I didn't know how to get out of that kind of a lie. I tried to blade the shot, and left it in the sand. The next week I got several hundred letters from TV viewers, explaining how to hit that shot.

"When I finally did get it onto the green, I was lying seven. I looked up at the television tower and there were Bing and several of my friends from NBC. I was so nervous I couldn't focus on the ball. I missed the ball completely with the putter and hit the toe of my shoe instead."

Singer Robert Goulet experienced the horrors of a duffer on TV the following year. Driving off the 16th tee, he toed a shot which nearly decapitated announcer Chris Schenkel in the tower at the 15th green. "I've seen bad shots," Schenkel laughed, "but never one that endangered my life."

On the 18th hole, Goulet scraped and hacked his way up the fairway with the cameras homing in on him. He heeled one shot off his left foot and took four to get out of a seawall trap. Attempting to laugh his anguish away, Goulet skipped over the gallery rope near the green, tripped and fell.

Nor have the pros been immune to the terrors of the coaxial cable. As Tommy Bolt was preparing to tee off on 17 one year at Pebble Beach, a young deer wandered out onto the fairway. Bolt stepped back. The deer left. When Tommy began to address the ball again, the deer reappeared. Bolt glared around and growled, "Where in hell are the marshals?"

As he was standing over a putt on the 18th green, Tommy's keen ears picked up the sound of a whirring camera. He stared menacingly at the TV tower, then realized the distraction was being created by an amateur photographer, a woman. Ambling over to the spectator, Bolt solicitously inquired, "Lady, why are you doing this to me? I wouldn't come into your kitchen and crack my knuckles if you was makin' biscuits!"

The networks first arrived at the Crosby in 1958, when CBS did the telecast. The next year ABC took it. The mechanics of TV coverage weren't quite as sophisticated in those days. Needing a zoom lens for the camera on the 18th hole, ABC opted to fly one up from Los Angeles on the morning of the telecast. A fog delayed the arrival of the flight, and the local sheriff volunteered to meet the plane at the Monterey Airport and hurry the missing lens out to Pebble Beach. Network officials were nervously scanning the skies for the aircraft, which finally landed. The lens was installed two minutes before the tournament went on the air.

That was the year air time was running out as Art Wall, the leader, and Gene Littler, one stroke behind him, were coming up the 18th fairway together. When Littler hooked his second shot into the ocean, Bing hurriedly proclaimed Wall the winner just before sign-off.

In 1962, the year snow fell on Saturday night and postponed the final round a day, ABC had fun with the delay. It carried a half-hour show from the 18th green at Pebble Beach featuring a lively snowball fight between actor Dennis O'Keefe and several pros, coupled with a charming shot of Winnie Palmer watching in amusement from the window of Arnold's room at the Del Monte Lodge.

Dave Marr, who has since become a popular TV analyst for ABC, made his debut behind the microphones at the Crosby in 1967, on a cold and rainy day. "I had missed the cut," Marr recalls, "and Chris asked me to stick around and do some commentary. They put me at the 17th green, right on the ocean. I wore thermal underwear and a stocking cap and lord knows how many coats, and I about froze to death. I thought at the time there was not enough money on earth to make this worthwhile."

The constant problem for television is the possibility of a tie and sudden-death play-off, running the show beyond its scheduled air time. It happened in 1968, 1972 and 1973. Orville Moody stood on the 18th green in 1973 needing only a 2½ foot putt to beat Jack Nicklaus and Raymond Floyd by a stroke. Having finished a short TV interview, Floyd was about to leave for the airport. "Better wait around for a minute," advised his amateur partner, Clint Eastwood. "This guy has about one yip left."

Moody blew the putt and Nicklaus won the play-off with a birdie on the first extra hole.

In 1975 ABC brought a staff of 110 in addition to sixty local workers hired to help with scorekeeping in the monitor control

Expanding its bases from the traditional towers behind greens and tees, TV coverage of tournament golf has become mobile. Bob Rosburg (opposite page) wanders everywhere with his wireless mike, followed by a cameraman with portable equipment.

Jack Nicklaus holes a birdie putt to win the sudden-death play-off of the 1973 Crosby and accepts congratulations from happy caddie Angelo Argea and crestfallen foe Orville Moody.

booth. There were seventeen cameras stationed at Pebble Beach, plus a wireless camera that followed Bob Rosburg and his wireless mike around on the course.

"We thought we were ready for just about anything last year," says Chuck Howard, the ABC producer. "Then Gene Littler, who was playing his third round at Cypress Point, shot 68 and took the lead."

The ABC crew had to hurry over to Cypress with a portable equipment unit to shoot Littler on a few holes, inserting the videotape into its live broadcast from Pebble.

The result was considerably more successful than a similar project undertaken a few years earlier by NBC. "We wanted to tape Bing interviewing some of the golfers at Spyglass early in the tournament," recalls Don Ellis, an NBC producer. "We spent a whole morning over there, then discovered the recording device had been malfunctioning. I'll never forget Bing's reaction. He shrugged and said, 'Well, it was a nice place to while away a few hours. Let's do it over.'"

Ever since his tournament became a network show, Crosby has donated his time as commentator. He also has been instrumental in maintaining a long-running affiliation with his sponsors, principally 3M and Oldsmobile.

"I've enjoyed my television work at the tournament despite the years of nasty weather," Crosby says. "It gets pretty cold up in that tower. There were times when we laced our coffee with a drop or two of the grape."

Bing was hospitalized during the 1974 tournament, but returned in 1975, chipper as ever, adding his own articulate flavor to the proceedings. Observing him, Wells

Twombly wrote in the San Francisco *Examiner:*

Just as the television network's electronic shock troops turned on their cameras, this massive fog bank came creeping across the waters of Carmel Bay, blotting out the glorious sunshine. Several golfers, coming down from the upland meadows, disappeared from view. A damp mist began to fall. Women who had exchanged pants suits for skirts went shivering back to the lodge, their legs turned an appropriate blue in the deepening chill. People began to huddle under umbrellas, and up in the ABC booth, the patron saint of this most unique of golfing events pulled the collar of his coat up around his expensive tonsils.

The Pros: Curtain Call for the Stars

The prospect of spending four days on the golf course in the company of amateur partners has never held a strong appeal for the touring pros. They feel a good deal more comfortable at work with their peers away from the distractions and the fumbling frivolity so often generated in pro-am events.

But the Crosby traditionally has been an enjoyable stop on the tour, for reasons that transcend the three excellent golf courses, the sizable purse and the presence of Bing.

For one thing, many of the pros select their amateur partners. The pairs compete as teams through the first 54 holes of the tournament and, if they are among the 25 low qualifiers, in the final round as well.

The format is unlike the Bob Hope Desert Classic, where the pros are paired with different amateurs each of the first four rounds, an ordeal that often tests even the most tolerant of the personalities on tour. A fifth round for pros only ends the Hope.

Through the years the Crosby has been characterized by great champions. It has been won twenty-seven times by players who have won at least one of the four major championships—the U.S. and British opens, the Masters and the PGA. Among them have been Sam Snead, who has won three Crosbys and tied for a fourth; Jack Nicklaus, a three-time winner, and Ben Hogan.

Nicklaus has attained more success at Pebble Beach than any golfer in history. He won the U. S. Amateur there in 1961, the U. S. Open in 1972 and the Crosby in 1967, 1972 and 1973. Since turning pro in 1962, he has competed in the Crosby for fourteen straight years.

"I like Pebble Beach, obviously,"

Nicklaus says. "But it goes deeper than that. My pro-am partner is always Bob Hoag. He's a relaxing guy to play with, and the Crosby gives him a chance to get out of those Ohio winters and hit a few shots in front of the galleries."

Hoag is an insurance executive from Columbus, a 6-handicap member at Scioto Country Club, where Nicklaus learned to play. "He's ten years older than I am," Jack says, "and occasionally he becomes a calming influence in tight spots."

Nicklaus has been involved in a few. In 1967 he broke away from a tie with Arnold Palmer early in the final round, on his twenty-seventh birthday, for a back-nine 31 that included birdies on 12, 13, 14, 16 and 17. He beat Johnny Miller with a birdie putt on the first play-off hole in 1972, and won a three-man play-off with Raymond Floyd and Orville Moody in 1973 with a birdie putt on the same hole.

The Crosby, ironically, is one of the few tournaments of consequence that Palmer has never won, although he finished second in 1966 and 1971, third in 1967 and fourth in 1961. Arnold's best showing in the pro-am was a tie for third in 1966 with his manager, Mark McCormack, who was his regular partner in the Crosby for fifteen years.

"You go into the Crosby knowing that the show business people are going to clown around a little," Palmer says. "I learned to accept that a long time ago. The fans like to watch them, and they add a lot to the tournament."

The pros have also benefited financially from business ventures initiated by their contact at the Crosby with corporate heads and other assorted tycoons of industry.

Among the more permanent teams in Crosby history have been, in addition to

Nicklaus-Hoag and Palmer-McCormack, Byron Nelson and Ed Lowery, Cary Middlecoff and Ed Crowley, Jack Burke and George Coleman, Bobby Nichols and Glen Campbell, Bob Rosburg and John Brodie, and Bob Lunn and Nelson Cullenward. Brodie helped Rosburg 37 strokes during their pro-am win in 1970.

There have been five pros who have swept the individual championship and shared in the pro-am title with amateur partners—Snead in 1937, Leland Gibson in 1942, Art Wall in 1959, Johnny Pott in 1968 and Johnny Miller in 1974.

The tournament record for 72 holes of competition is 277, set by Billy Casper in 1958. Oddly enough, it was the first year the format was expanded from 54 holes.

Incidents of discord have, inevitably, surfaced occasionally. Notable was the time years ago on the 16th hole at Cypress Point, when Clayton Heafner's partner, playing horribly, asked the sulking Heafner whether he should go for the green or play it safe.

"Neither," growled Heafner. "Pick up the ball and put it in your pocket."

Another pro was equally unhappy over the performance of his partner, a celebrity

Not even three-time champ Jack Nicklaus is immune to the Crosby's sandy hazards. Above, in 1966, he pitches

widely recognized for drinking on the course. "Your breath is so strong," the pro fumed, "that if you blew it on the tomb of the Unknown Soldier, he'd jump up and play thirty-six holes."

Nor have the problems always been confined to the golf course. In 1971 Doug Sanders and his partner, Ken Schnitzer of Houston, awakened in their Monterey hotel to discover a thief had stolen $24,886 worth of jewelry. Among the missing items was a set of silver cuff links presented Sanders by his pal, then Vice-President Spiro Agnew.

The chances of a medium-handicap amateur making the cut are usually dictated by the varying fortunes of his pro. In 1972 Ken Towns, a California pro, was paired with Wendell Anderson, the Minnesota governor. Towns struggled to an 85 in the opening round at Pebble Beach and two days later set a course record of 66 at Spyglass. Despite a best-ball score of 59 that day, the team missed the cut.

Once the pro-am cut is made after 54 holes, the final round invariably has been dominated by the battle for first place among the contending pros, and there have been some memorable finishes.

up from the beach on 16th at Cypress. At right, in 1973, he works on a bunker shot on 16th at Pebble Beach.

In 1959 Art Wall had a 5-stroke lead over Gene Littler with four holes to play. Littler birdied twice and Wall bogeyed twice, and Wall's slender one-stroke lead on the 18th wasn't secure until Littler hooked his second shot into the ocean.

Rosburg birdied the 18th from twelve feet in 1961 to win, moments after Roberto de Vicenzo missed his try for an eagle putt that would have tied him for the lead and minutes before Bill Collins fell out of a first-place tie with bogeys on the last two holes.

Billy Casper waited patiently in the press room in 1963 as Nicklaus and Bob Duden three-putted the 72nd hole to cost themselves a share of Casper's lead, Duden missing a four-footer with an odd-looking pendulum putter he had built himself.

"If Duden had won the tournament with that putter," remarked Casper, "it would have set golf back one hundred years."

The 1975 Crosby lacked a close finish, but it did produce one of its most popular champions in forty-four-year-old Gene Littler, who underwent surgery for cancer less than three years before. Littler led by 4 shots after 54 holes and maintained that margin in treacherous winds the final day.

"This tournament means a lot to me," he said quietly. "I've been trying to win it since 1954. It proved I could come back after my little setback and win on a great golf course."

Three views of the Crosby. Jack Burke parts the rough in search of a lost ball. Bill Collins catches a quick nap on the practice green after a 67 at Pebble Beach and Arnold Palmer's birdie putt prompts a joyous response from his caddie.

Through it all, the pros have contributed much more than their shot-making skills. Despite the pressure of big money, they have injected their own flavor of humor.

Surveying a putt from all angles one day, Chi Chi Rodriguez finally asked his caddie which way it would break.

"Toward the ocean, always toward the ocean," replied the caddie.

"Yeah," grunted Rodriguez, "but which one—the Atlantic or the Pacific?"

Dave Marr once consoled a fellow pro who had become disconsolate over his deteriorating game. "Don't worry," Marr smiled. "What you've developed is only a terminal slice."

Not even Crosby himself has been immune from an occasional needle. Several years ago, in the midst of a particularly rough round, Tommy Bolt approached the 13th green and shook his club in defiance at the home where Bing then lived.

"I'm gonna get that crooner out on this golf course," Bolt thundered, "and make him play the 8th, 9th and 10th holes over and over until he pars them all."

Rough going at the Crosby. Bert Yancey in deep trouble at Cypress Point.

THE
EPILOGUE

1937

SAM'S SOGGY VICTORY

Sam Snead's 68 on a water-logged course will always be remembered as the winning score of the first Crosby, but the most remarkable aspect of Bing's opening venture into tournament golf sponsorship was that it was held at all.

Between the foul weather and the political intrigue within the councils of the PGA, the chances of launching the $3,000 Rancho Santa Fe Amateur-Pro, as it was called then, were quite remote.

Lawson Little, the former two-time U. S. and British Amateur champion, had entered as a professional. He had not yet joined the PGA, however, and the Southern California PGA section protested his entry.

Crosby, a novice in these matters, turned for support to Fred Corcoran, the PGA tournament director who was having problems of his own. Corcoran had been named by the PGA to replace the ousted Bob Harlow as tournament director only a few months earlier, and already a bloc of prominent pros, led by Horton Smith, wanted Corcoran out and Harlow back in.

A series of noisy meetings preceded Little's acceptance, but Lawson was delayed in Los Angeles working on a golf film and arrived too late to enter.

Rains washed out the first round and threatened to drown the entire tournament. Sunday dawned clear, however, and Snead splashed around the course in a 36–32, without a single bogey, to win by 4 strokes. Sam also shared first place in the pro-am and proclaimed himself "$762.30 richer than when I teed off."

Sam Snead

Professional

Sam Snead	—68	$500
George Von Elm	—72	350
Leonard Dodson	—73	181
Henry Picard	—73	181
Jim Fogerty	—73	181
Fay Coleman	—73	181
Denny Shute	—74	65
Stanley Kertes	—74	65
Frank Stuhler	—74	65
Willie Goggin	—74	65
Sam Parks, Jr.	—74	65

Pro-Am

Sam Snead—George Lewis	—68
Fay Coleman—Jim Pierce	—68
Tony Joy—Richard Arlen	—69
Jimmy Hines—Forrest Braddock	—69
Herman Keiser—Tom Meanley	—70
Walter Schrieber—Johnny Dawson	—70
Jim Fogerty—S. F. McLeod	—70
William Kawall—Don Gibson	—70
Stan Kertes—Bert Allenberg	—70
Willie Hunter—Gregory LaCava	—71
Fred Sherman—Andy Borthwick	—71
Sam Parks, Jr.—R. J. Compton	—71
Lloyd Mangrum—Guy Showley	—71
Harold Sampson—Bob Fahy	—71
Bill Jelliffe—C. J. Roberts	—71

1938

ORANGES
FOR
LUNCH

Sam Snead became a two-time champion in the Crosby's second year by overtaking Jimmy Hines and Jimmy Demaret on the final round with a Rancho Santa Fe course record 67 for a 36-hole total of 139.

Hines shot a closing 72 for 141 and Demaret, entertaining the gallery with his quips despite the fact his game was a bit shaky, had 74 for 142.

In a welcome contrast from the first Crosby, the weather was sunny and warm, the shrubbery on the course bursting in color.

"The oranges were just turning ripe that week," recalled Demaret. "We weren't making much money playing golf in those days, and many of us plucked our lunch off the orange trees bordering several fairways."

Art Bell, an Hawaiian-born pro from San Francisco, teamed with one of his Midwick Country Club members, Phil Finlay, to win the pro-am with 134, beating Snead and Doug McKinnon by a stroke. Finlay, a former NCAA champion who played to a 1-handicap, had two birdies on the back line of the second round.

Lawson Little disqualified himself from the pro competition when he spotted an error on his card after he had signed it. He was allowed to remain in the pro-am, and tied for sixth.

Sam Snead

Professional			Pro-Am	
Sam Snead	72-67—139	$500	Art Bell—Phil Finlay	—134
Jimmy Hines	69-72—141	350	Sam Snead—Doug McKinnon	—135
Jimmy Demaret	68-74—142	250	Willie Hunter—Jerry Stone	—136
Horton Smith	73-70—143	175	Jimmy Hines—Cliff Roberts	—137
Henry Picard	72-71—143	175	Charles Lacey—Bert Allenberg	—137
Willie Hunter	73-71—144	112	Mat Kowal—Don Boyen	—138
Al Zimmerman	72-72—144	112	Lawson Little—Dutch Shaffer	—138
Ben Hogan	74-71—145	75	Al Zimmerman—F. J. Anson	—138
Dick Metz	71-75—146	50	Jimmy Demaret—John McCorkie	—139
John Revolta	73-73—146	50	George Schneiter—Darsie L. Darsie	—139
			Ben Hogan—Braven Dyer	—139
			Marvin Stahl—William McIntyre	—139
			Charles Dogdon—Rudy Holm	—139

1939

BALLAD FOR A COUNTRY BOY

With Sam Snead absent from the tournament in 1939, due to the illness of his mother back in West Virginia, his place in the winners' circle was taken by another country boy.

E. J. ("Dutch") Harrison, a product of the Arkansas hills, outlasted Byron Nelson and Horton Smith in a tense finish to win the $500 first-place prize with 69-69—138.

Nelson opened the tournament by 3-putting the first green and then firing 68, adding a 71 the second day. Smith reversed that order, closing fast with a 68 that pushed Harrison right down to his final putt.

Maurie Luxford, Bing's close friend from the Lakeside Golf Club who had become a Crosby tournament official, played a double role by teaming with pro Johnny Revolta to win the pro-am with 63 on the final round for 130.

One of the prime gallery favorites was the only woman in the field, Babe Didrikson Zaharias. Babe's partner was her husband, George Zaharias. They were never in contention, but her appearance would be fondly remembered by Bing thirty-five years later when he made an unsuccessful effort to have women pros included in the Crosby on the Monterey Peninsula.

"Babe added a lot to the tournament," Bing declared. "She hit it as far as some of the men pros."

Dutch Harrison

Professional

Dutch Harrison	69-69—138	$500
Byron Nelson	68-71—139	300
Horton Smith	71-68—139	300
Bill Nary	70-70—140	175
Jim McHale	69-71—140	175
Ben Hogan	69-72—141	112
John Revolta	74-67—141	112
Lloyd Mangrum	70-72—142	50
Jimmy Hines	72-70—142	50
Earl Martin	71-71—142	50
Harry Cooper	72-70—142	50

Pro-Am

John Revolta—Maurie Luxford	—130
Bill Nary—F. P. Hixon	—131
Fred Sherman—A. J. Borthwick	—131
Charles Lacey—Bert Allenberg	—131
Ben Hogan—Bud McCrary	—132
Dutch Harrison—Capt. A. B. Webster	—132

Johnny Revolta

Bing on the 16th tee at Cypress, where he scored his hole-in-one in 1947.

A scenic vantage point at Spyglass, where author Robert Louis Stevenson once dreamed of pirates.

Fun time for the galleries: following the celebrities.
Bob Hope, happy with a long putt; Jack Lemmon,
laboring over a chip shot; and Tennessee Ernie Ford
(opposite page) entertaining his audience.

A pair of popular ABC Crosby regulars. Chris Schenkel (top photo) smiles for the camera, and Jim McKay in the tower above the 15th green at Pebble Beach.

Jack Nicklaus, on center stage with ABC's Frank Gifford, in the tent "studio" behind the 18th green at Pebble.

Portrait of a champion: Gene Littler finally wins his first Crosby after twenty years.

Porky Oliver, who made headlines thirteen years later in the Crosby with a 16 on a par-3 hole, attained his first national recognition in the 1940 tournament.

After opening with 68, the portly Oliver birdied the first three holes of the final round and shot 67 for a 135 that held off Vic Ghezzi by 3 strokes.

In a prophetic observation, syndicated columnist Henry McLemore paid Oliver this tribute:

The Crosby has become the cradle of champions. Nobody took Sam Snead seriously when he showed up in 1937, and he won the tournament twice. Last year Dutch Harrison arrived at Rancho Santa Fe with a patched-up set of clubs and an empty stomach, and he beat the field.

When Porky Oliver got here this year all that was known about him was that he could out-eat any five men in the game. He had never won a tournament of consequence, but he proved he could play with anyone in the game by winning this Crosby.

Five months later, Oliver, in contention for a U. S. Open championship, was disqualified for teeing off ahead of schedule in the final round.

John Geertsen, who would become one of the most successful teaching pros on the West Coast, won the pro-am with Russ Osgood with 129.

Porky Oliver

Professional

Porky Oliver	68-67—135	$500.00
Vic Ghezzi	69-69—138	350.00
Harold McSpaden	68-71—139	225.00
Ben Hogan	71-68—139	225.00
Willie Goggin	69-71—140	150.00
*Bruce McCormick	72-68—140	
Rut Coffey	71-70—141	67.85
Sam Byrd	69-72—141	67.85
Stan Kertes	71-70—141	67.85
Lloyd Mangrum	70-71—141	67.85
John Geertsen	70-71—141	67.85
Toney Penna	69-72—141	67.85
Ralph Guldahl	69-72—141	67.85
*Wilford Wehrie	73-68—141	

* Amateurs

Pro-Am

John Geertsen—Russ Osgood	—129
Ky Laffoon—Pat Abbott	—130
Sam Byrd—Tom McAvity	—131
Willie Goggin—Marshall Duffield	—131
Harold McSpaden—Ed Lowery	—132
Chick Rutan—Ford Palmer	—132
John Thoren—Paul Gardner	—132
Craig Wood—Wilford Wehrie	—132
Fay Coleman—Dick Pugh	—132
Porky Oliver—Dr. Hugh Strathearn	—133

1941

WHAT'S A DYNASTY?

The field had grown to 319 players in 1941—so many that the opening round had to be spread over two days. Sam Snead won again, for the third time in four years, with 67-69—136 that edged Craig Wood by a stroke.

Porky Oliver, apparently unfrayed by a couple of hectic cross-country auto tours, led the first round with 66, using borrowed clubs.

Oliver left by car immediately after the Oakland Open to drive home to Wilmington, Delaware, to appear before his draft board. His father, believing Porky to be through playing golf for the duration, took the clubs out of the car and put them in the woodshed.

After receiving a temporary deferment from the draft board, Porky drove to the Crosby tournament and discovered the clubs were missing.

A 75 on the final round bumped Porky out of the picture. Wood just missed a twelve-foot putt on the last hole which would have tied Snead.

Leonard Dodson brought a strong amateur, Ray Watson of Kansas City, who helped him on 15 strokes as they won the team competition at 124—20 under par.

Press accounts of the tournament noted the appearance of a player named Ernie Sabayrac, labeling him "the shortest pro in the game." The five-foot Sabayrac is today president of his own golf apparel distributing company.

Professional

Sam Snead	67-69—136	$500
Craig Wood	69-68—137	350
Bill Nary	67-71—138	237
Harold McSpaden	69-69—138	237
Ben Hogan	69-70—139	125
Byron Nelson	68-71—139	125
Leonard Dodson	70-69—139	125
Lloyd Mangrum	69-70—139	125
Jimmy Demaret	70-69—139	125
Emery Zimmerman	72-68—140	16
Johnny Bulla	74-66—140	16
John Revolta	72-68—140	16

Pro-Am

Leonard Dodson—Ray Watson	—124
Lloyd Mangrum—Nelson Hill	—130
Harold McSpaden—Ed Lowery	—131
John Bulla—Johnny Weissmuller	—131
Jimmy Demaret—Pete Watta	—131
Felix Seratin—Johnny Dawson	—131
Ray Hill—Gerry Bert	—132
Ben Hogan—Bob Gardner	—132
Toney Penna—Bud Ward	—132
Byron Nelson—George Ward	—133
George Fazio—Dr. Hugh Strathearn	—133
Craig Wood—Marshall Duffield	—133
Dutch Harrison—Wilford Wehrie	—133

Sam Snead

1942

AN AMATEUR SHOWS HOW

The Crosby tournament programs list the 1942 co-champions as Lloyd Mangrum and Leland Gibson, but the fact is that Bing's valedictory at Rancho Santa Fe was won by an amateur.

Johnny Dawson, a scratch handicap at the Lakeside Golf Club in Hollywood, was 11 under par with 66-67—133 to beat Mangrum and Gibson by 3 shots.

The U. S. Golf Association had barred Dawson from its U. S. Amateur for twelve years because of his affiliation with a sporting goods firm, but Dawson maintained he was still an amateur and declined the $800 first-place money from the purse which was boosted to $5,000.

Dawson's pro partner, Harry Cooper, shot 72-75. Cooper helped his amateur, an ironic twist, on just 6 of the 36 holes for a winning pro-am team score of 127.

Mangrum made a good run at Dawson the final round with 66, a figure matched by Sam Snead in a foursome with Bing Crosby, Bob Hope and Ben Hogan. Sam, however, had shot an opening 77.

It was a wartime Clambake, and the last one ever held at Rancho. The tournament would be resumed five years later in a new setting on the Monterey Peninsula.

Johnny Dawson

Harry Cooper

Professional			Pro-Am	
*John Dawson	66-67—133		Harry Cooper—John Dawson	—127
Lloyd Mangrum	70-66—136	$700	Leland Gibson—L. A. Nicholetti	—130
Leland Gibson	67-69—136	700	Herb Tolson—Ralph Wolf	—130
Herman Barron	70-67—137	475	Horton Smith—Bob Gardner	—131
Joe Brown	68-70—138	375	Willie Goggin—Ted Hobgood	—131
Willie Goggin	72-67—139	300	Lloyd Mangrum—Nelson Hill	—131
Herman Keiser	68-72—140	225	Sam Snead—Bing Crosby	—132
Ralph Guldahl	68-72—140	225	Frank Rodia—Pete Apratto	—132
Frank Rodia	71-70—141	113	Herman Keiser—Nate Marshall	—132
Jimmy Hines	69-72—141	113	Ray Hill—Gene O'Neill	—133
George Fazio	70-71—141	113	Joe Brown—Al Farmer	—133
Ray Mangrum	69-72—141	113	Ralph Guldahl—Cliff Garner	—133
Les Kennedy	71-70—141	113	Harold McSpaden—Ed Lowery	—133

* Amateur

1947

WELCOME TO PEBBLE BEACH

Bing resumed his tournament in 1947 and moved it north to the Monterey Peninsula. Some of the old informality of Rancho Santa Fe was lost in the transition, but the precedent for exciting finishes and bad weather continued, and new traditions were established.

Tournament proceeds were channeled to charity for the first time; the competition was expanded to 54 holes over the Pebble Beach, Monterey Peninsula Country Club and Cypress Point courses; and the purse was doubled from $5,000 to $10,000.

The professional co-champions were George Fazio and Ed Furgol with scores of 213, Furgol grabbing his share of first place with a 5-iron shot into the cup for an eagle deuce on the 16th hole at Pebble Beach on the final round. Furgol then parred in through a driving rain for 72.

"I thought I had it won until Ed's eagle," Fazio was to say later. "They had a big Calcutta, and there was a lot of celebrating among Furgol's buyers. People who never drank before were guzzling whiskey that night."

Sam Snead and Roger Kelly overcame some friction on the first tee on opening day—a discord initiated by the fact Kelly had been drinking—to collaborate for the pro-am championship with 196.

Bing hit his approach shot on 18 into the trees at Cypress Point on the first round. Gazing sorrowfully at his ball, wedged between two branches, he inquired, "Where's Johnny Weissmuller?"

George Fazio

Ed Furgol

Roger Kelly

Professional

George Fazio	68-70-75—213	$1,625
Ed Furgol	72-69-72—213	1,625
Lloyd Mangrum	72-68-76—216	734
Newt Bassler	71-74-71—216	734
Sam Snead	76-70-70—216	734
Ed Oliver	70-70-77—217	350
Ellsworth Vines	71-70-76—217	350
Dick Metz	67-73-79—219	150
Johnny Bulla	72-73-75—220	150
Jimmy Demaret	74-69-77—220	150

Pro-Am

Sam Snead—Roger Kelly	—196
Al Zimmerman—Bud Ward	—199
Newt Bassler—F. A. Hennekin	—199
Ed Furgol—Bill Higgins	—200
Jim Milward—Don Edwards	—203
Dick Metz—Fred Dold	—204
Harold McSpaden—Ed Lowery	—204
George Payton—Jack Anderson	—204
Johnny Bulla—Del Webb	—204
George Fazio—Milt Wershow	—205
Toney Penna—Edgar Kennedy	—205

1948

PUTTING THE BADGE ON BING

Much of the fun took place off the golf courses in 1948. Lloyd Mangrum won the tournament by 5 strokes with 205, despite putting in some long evening sessions at the Blue Ox and Biff's El Estero, a couple of lively niteries which are no more.

Bing was made an honorary chief of police by the city of Monterey, "to serve in such office until such time as he can no longer dance the fandango, swing a golf club or serenade the senoritas." With the honor went all the prerogatives of office, including the right for Bing and his horses to take their siestas in the city jail.

It was the first year of the Golf Clinic, held on the second tee at Pebble Beach, which became a long-running annual feature at the Crosby. Lawson Little served as master of ceremonies and the pros showed how to swing properly. Ben Hogan, who displayed the grip and stance, even clowned it up with some gag shots.

Hogan and Johnny Dawson won the pro-am with 197, teaming for 3 birdies on the last four holes. Mangrum finished with 68 at Pebble Beach, which played most difficult because of the rare appearance of an east wind, blowing shots toward the ocean.

Lloyd Mangrum

Ben Hogan

Professional

Lloyd Mangrum	70-67-68—205	$2,000
Stan Leonard	71-67-72—210	1,250
Ben Hogan	72-69-70—211	1,000
Bobby Locke	73-69-70—212	700
Johnny Palmer	75-66-75—216	450
Jack Burke	75-70-71—216	450
Cary Middlecoff	77-71-69—217	225
Jimmy Demaret	73-70-74—217	225
Martin Pose	71-69-78—218	150
Charles Congdon	74-68-77—219	100
George Fazio	70-72-77—219	100
Art Bell	75-68-76—219	100
Vic Ghezzi	73-71-75—219	100
Jim Ferrier	73-70-76—219	100

Pro-Am

Ben Hogan–Johnny Dawson	—197
Chandler Harper–Warner Keeley	—199
Bobby Locke–Frank Stranahan	—199
Lloyd Mangrum–Bob Simmers	—199
Stan Leonard–T. Suffern Tailer	—200
Herman Keiser–Bob Gardner	—202
Skip Alexander–Morgan Fottrell	—202
Jimmy Demaret–Dan Searle	—203
Cary Middlecoff–Billy Hoelle	—204
Enrique Bertolino–Bill Higgins	—204
Vic Ghezzi–Nate Marshall	—204
Ralph Hutchinson–Millard Jones	—204

1949

THE
HAWK
FLIES
HIGH

It was the only time Ben Hogan would ever win the individual competition in the Crosby, but he did it in typical Hogan style, coming from behind with 70 at Pebble Beach on the final round for a 54-hole total of 208.

Two weeks later, en route by car from Phoenix to his home in Fort Worth, Hogan collided with a bus and suffered multiple injuries which sidelined him for the remainder of the year.

He had entered the Crosby in a particularly resolute frame of mind, following an unsatisfactory showing a week earlier at Los Angeles. Hogan showed how ready he was by shooting 63 in a practice round at Cypress Point.

After 36 holes, however, the leader was amateur Frank Stranahan, the weight-lifting muscleman, who shot 66 at Monterey Peninsula on the second day for 137, one stroke ahead of Hogan.

The putting miseries that became so evident later in Hogan's career nagged him throughout the Crosby. He three-putted seven times, including three the final round, but he also had 3 birdie deuces over the last 18. "When old Blue Blades makes up his mind," noted Bing, "then it's just good night. That's all brother."

Syndicated columnist Grantland Rice provided the Crosby with a meaningful tribute when he called it "the greatest golf tournament in the world."

In the pro-am, San Francisco natives Bill Nary and baseball manager Lefty O'Doul added a nice local touch by winning with 196.

Bing Crosby and Ben Hogan

Bill Nary and Lefty O'Doul

Professional				Pro-Am	
Ben Hogan	70-68-70—208	$2,000		Bill Nary—Lefty O'Doul	—196
Jim Ferrier	69-70-71—210	1,250		John Barnum—Harrison Goodwin	—198
Jimmy Demaret	69-70-72—211	1,000		Ben Hogan—John Dawson	—199
Bill Nary	66-73-74—213	700		Jimmy Demaret—Warren Ingersoll	—200
Emery Zimmerman	71-70-73—214	450		Emery Zimmerman—Doug Lewis	—200
Joe Brown	68-73-73—214	450		Cary Middlecoff—Frank Stranahan	—201
Chick Harbert	69-73-73—215	300		Jim Ferrier—Forrest Tucker	—202
Art Bell	73-72-71—216	150		Art Bell—Tom Dwyer	—202
Lew Worsham	72-69-75—216	150		Sam Snead—Roger Kelly	—203
Cary Middlecoff	76-65-75—216	150		Lawson Little—Billy Hoelle	—203
				Ellsworth Vines—Dave Taylor	—203
				Ed Furgol—George Coleman	—203
				Chick Harbert—Dan Searle	—203

1950

FOUR
FOR
THE
MONEY

Although he finished 9 strokes out of the lead, 7 over par and 2 out of the money, Ben Hogan was the focal point of the 1950 Crosby.

It was the second tournament of Hogan's comeback following a long hospitalization and recuperation from multiple injuries suffered in an automobile-bus collision the previous February.

Hogan had tied for the Los Angeles Open championship with Sam Snead the week before the Crosby. Bad weather washed out their 18-hole play-off, so they had to return to Los Angeles three days after the Crosby was over. Snead won that play-off, and it was evident at the Crosby that Ben had a long way to go before fully regaining his strength and stamina.

"Right now I just can't keep up the pace," Hogan said following rounds of 77-74-72 at the Crosby. But the galleries poured out to watch him, cheering his eagle 3 on the 6th at Pebble Beach, the final round.

Snead had a big gallery at Pebble Beach, too, including film star Esther Williams, whose husband, Ben Gage, was playing in another foursome. Sam missed an eight-foot putt on the 18th green and wound up in a four-way tie for first place at 214 with Smiley Quick, Dave Douglas and Jack Burke. This was before the Crosby had sudden-death play-offs.

Marty Furgol and Don Edwards shared the pro-am at 201 with the team of Ralph Blomquist and Bud Moe.

Bing's four sons watched the tournament from a tree overhanging the 13th green. "They had some very strange stories to tell," Bing related, "about the play on that hole."

Sam Snead, Smiley Quick, Dave Douglas and Jack Burke, Jr.

Professional			Pro-Am	
Jack Burke, Jr.	75-67-72—214	$1,237	Ralph Blomquist—Bud Moe	—201
Dave Douglas	71-73-70—214	1,237	Marty Furgol—Don Edwards	—201
Sam Snead	69-72-73—214	1,237	Dave Douglas—John Weissmuller	—202
Smiley Quick	72-69-73—214	1,237	Jackson Bradley—Leo Durocher	—205
Dutch Harrison	74-70-73—217	450	Fred Haas—Howard Parker	—205
Fred Haas	74-69-74—217	450	Fred Hawkins—Ed Flynn	—205
Fred Hawkins	72-73-74—219	225	Bud Ward—Ralph Kiner	—205
Ralph Blomquist	73-71-75—219	225	Ed Vines—C. Pardee Erdman	—206
Ray Gafford	73-74-73—220	133	Sherm Elworthy—Alan Patee	—206
Jackson Bradley	73-72-75—220	133	Byron Nelson—Ed Lowery	—206
Cary Middlecoff	74-68-78—220	133	Bob Watson—Tom Ray, Jr.	—206

1951

LAST BOW FOR LORD BYRON

He hadn't won a tour ever since the Chicago Victory Open at Medinah in July of 1946. He was a rancher now, through with the nerve-wracking grind of tournament golf. The Crosby was just a social visit for him, to see some friends from the old days.

So Byron Nelson went out and beat par in all three rounds and shot 209 to win the 1951 Crosby by 3 strokes, the fourth straight year that a Texan had won it or shared first place.

Byron was only thirty-eight, but he had not played the tour in four years. His championships in the Masters, U. S. Open and PGA seemed to be in the distant past, and his string of eleven straight tournament victories in 1945 came in another era, when they paid off in war bonds.

"I've got some cows to tend down in Texas," said Nelson after the Crosby. "I'm not going back on the tour." And he never did, on a regular basis.

Nelson's domination of the pro competition was more mechanical than theatrical, but Phil Harris contributed the entertainment by sinking a ninety-foot birdie putt on the 17th hole at Pebble Beach to win the pro-am with Dutch Harrison.

Almost forgotten is the fact that Harrison had hit his tee shot on 17 into the ocean. With the pressure on, Harris sliced a driver to the right front edge of the green. Then he rolled in the monster. "If Jack Benny had seen this," remarked Harris, who was the comedian's radio show bandleader at the time, "I'd have hit him for a raise."

Dutch Harrison

Byron Nelson

Phil Harris

Professional			Pro-Am	
Byron Nelson	71-67-71—209	$2,000	Dutch Harrison—Phil Harris	—196
Cary Middlecoff	76-67-69—212	1,250	Joe Kirkwood, Jr.—Ben Gage	—198
Ed Furgol	75-70-68—213	733	Ed Furgol—William Boyd	—200
George Fazio	71-71-71—213	733	Skee Riegel—Dr. John Johnston	—200
Julius Boros	72-72-69—213	733	Earl Stewart—Paul Gardner	—202
Joe Kirkwood, Jr.	71-70-73—214	400	Jack Burke, Jr.—George Coleman	—202
Smiley Quick	76-69-70—215	200	Cary Middlecoff—Ed Crowley	—202
Pete Cooper	70-73-72—215	200	Byron Nelson—Ed Lowery	—202
Jim Ferrier	70-73-72—215	200	Lew Worsham—Ralph Kiner	—203
Dutch Harrison	72-69-75—216	150	Bill Nary—Lefty O'Doul	—204
			Doug Ford—Charles de Limur	—204
			Jimmy Clark—Vern Stephens	—204
			Henry Ransom—Roger Kelly	—204

1952

AWAY
ALL
BOATS

"The weather was more fit for Johnny Weissmuller's swimming than my 5-iron," quipped Jimmy Demaret. "But for $2,500 I can stand a little moisture."

Demaret had just finished winning the 1952 Crosby, shortened by rain to 36 holes, and he was fondly fingering his two checks, $2,000 for winning the pro division with a score of 145, and $500 for taking third place in the pro-am with Bob Hope.

In one of the worst-weather Crosby tournaments ever, the jaunty Texas pro had shot 74 at Cypress Point in wind that reached gusts of forty-five miles per hour, sat out Saturday's canceled round and squished around Pebble Beach for a closing 71.

Demaret's margin in the pro competition was 2 strokes over Art Bell, later to become the head pro at Pebble Beach. Bell, however, teamed with Billy Hoelle to share first place in the pro-am with Bob Toski and Dr. Bob Knudson, thanks to Hoelle's miraculous net double eagle with a 135-yard trap shot on the final hole.

Hoelle had warmed up for that theatrical windup by holding out a forty-foot chip shot on the 7th hole, the shot that moved his team into contention for the first time.

Demaret went up to the microphone at the Clambake presentation dinner to sing a duet with the glamorous Monica Lewis and match quips with Buddy Hackett.

Despite the weather, over 8,000 people followed play on the final day and Bing wrote a check of $17,000 to charity.

Jimmy Demaret

Bob Toski and Dr. Bob Knudson

Billy Hoelle and Art Bell

Professional			Pro-Am	
Jimmy Demaret	74-71—145	$2,000	Art Bell–Billy Hoelle	—133
Art Bell	72-75—147	1,250	Bob Toski–Dr. Bob Knudson	—133
Doug Ford	78-70—148	1,000	Jimmy Demaret–Bob Hope	—134
Jim Ferrier	78-71—149	600	Earl Stewart–Ken Venturi	—136
Al Brosch	75-74—149	600	Stan Horne–Tom Dwyer	—137
Bob Toski	78-72—150	283	Byron Nelson–Ed Lowery	—137
Ev Goulart	77-73—150	283	Doug Ford–Jim French	—139
John Barnum	76-74—150	283	Marty Furgol–Stan More	—139
Earl Stewart	80-71—151	133	Jack Shields–Jim Saphier	—140
Lloyd Mangrum	79-72—151	133	Jack Burke, Jr.–George Coleman	—140
Al Besselink	79-72—151	133	Julius Boros–Charley Seaver	—140

1953

WHO NEEDS PALM SPRINGS?

The rumor spread like a grass fire through the 1953 Crosby that the tournament would be moved to a warm-weather site, probably Palm Springs. Bing squelched the story by remarking, "You wouldn't ask Laurence Olivier to perform in a bowling alley. No, this is da place."

It was the merriest and liveliest Crosby ever, with a turnout of 25,000 on Saturday and receipts for charity establishing a tournament record of $45,000. The Clambake dinner on Sunday night featured Rosemary Clooney, Phil Harris, Bob Hope and the Les Brown band, together with a few solos by Bing.

Lloyd Mangrum won the tournament with 204, 4 shots ahead of Julius Boros. It followed directly after Mangrum's 5-shot victory margin in the Los Angeles Open.

When Mangrum fluffed a few lines of his acceptance speech at the Clambake, Bing chided him. "You'd better get Doc Middlecoff to make you a new plate," said Crosby. Mangrum, no slouch as an ad libber, responded, "If I keep cashing checks like this, I'll get Doc a new plate."

The pro-am finished in a three-way tie at 190 between the teams of Cary Middlecoff-Ed Crowley, Gene Webb-Col. Ira Wintermute and Paul Runyan-Bob Vaillancourt.

Lloyd Mangrum

Gene Webb, Maurie Luxford, Col. Ira Wintermute

Professional			Pro-Am	
Lloyd Mangrum	67-66-71—204	$2,000	Cary Middlecoff—Ed Crowley	—190
Julius Boros	69-67-72—208	1,250	Gene Webb—Col. I. F. Wintermute	—190
Lawson Little	70-70-69—209	1,000	Paul Runyan—Bob Vaillancourt	—190
Johnny Bulla	70-68-72—210	533	Julius Boros—Jack Walsh	—193
Al Besselink	71-71-68—210	533	Willie Goggin—Billy Hoelle	—193
Cary Middlecoff	69-67-74—210	533	Max Evans—Wheeler Farish	—194
Jack Burke, Jr.	67-70-75—212	225	Lloyd Mangrum—Milt Wershow	—194
Doug Ford	68-73-71—212	225	Dutch Harrison—Phil Harris	—195
Earl Stewart, Jr.	73-72-68—213	108	Doug Ford—Charles de Limur	—195
Bill Nary	69-73-71—213	108	Tommy Bolt—Julie Bescos	—195
Dutch Harrison	72-71-70—213	108		
Jim Ferrier	67-69-77—213	108		
Jimmy Demaret	70-69-74—213	108		
Gene Webb	71-71-71—213	108		

1954

DUTCH TREAT

Dutch Harrison stood on the 18th tee at Pebble Beach in the gathering twilight, yawned and stretched his forty-four-year-old muscles. He had the rare luxury of being able to take a double bogey on the home hole and still win the Crosby.

Which is exactly what Harrison did.

Not even that tarnished finish, however, could spoil a memorable week for the tour veteran, whose 210 on rounds of 71-68-71 beat Jimmy Demaret by a stroke and Tommy Bolt by 2.

There was a four-way tie in the pro-am at 193 among the teams of Art Wall-Gene Littler, Walt Burkemo-Lefty O'Doul, Bud Ward-Harvie Ward and Doug Ford-Monty Moncrief. Littler, the reigning U. S. Amateur champion who was to turn pro a few weeks later, was making his first appearance in the Crosby.

On the final day, Bing cruised around Pebble Beach in a golf car accompanied by actress Mona Freeman. When he parked and walked up near the action at the 6th green, a gallery marshal approached him and said, "I'm sorry, sir, but you'll have to buy a ticket if you want to stay here."

Bing praised the marshal for his alertness, borrowed some money from a friend and bought the ticket.

Doug Ford, Monty Moncrief, Gene Littler, Art Wall

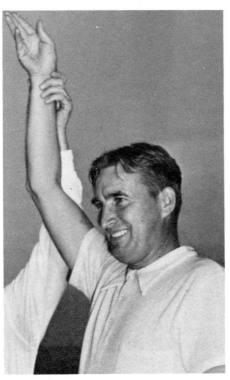

Dutch Harrison

Professional

Dutch Harrison	71-68-71—210	$2,000
Jimmy Demaret	73-68-70—211	1,250
Tommy Bolt	71-70-71—212	1,000
Doug Ford	71-71-71—213	700
Earl Stewart, Jr.	74-70-70—214	450
Peter Thomson	73-70-71—214	450
Jimmy Clark	69-74-73—216	200
Bob Toski	72-71-73—216	200
Walter Burkemo	74-71-71—216	200
Max Evans	77-67-73—217	112
Art Doering	69-76-72—217	112
Bob Rosburg	71-74-72—217	112
Lloyd Mangrum	73-70-74—217	112

Pro-Am

Bud Ward—Harvie Ward	—193
Walter Burkemo—Lefty O'Doul	—193
Art Wall, Jr.—Gene Littler	—193
Doug Ford—Monty Moncrief	—193
Peter Thomson—Gen. Robert McClure	—195
Bill Nary—Jeff Priddy	—196
Shelley Mayfield—Jack Cendoya	—196
Fred Hawkins—Bones Hamilton	—197
Art Bell—Billy Hoelle	—197
Vic Ghezzi—Nick Hilton	—197

1955

IT BEATS PULLING TEETH

"Before I went to bed last night," Cary Middlecoff was saying on the morning of the final round, "I had a wee spot of medicinal bourbon to quiet my nerves. And when I got up today I gave myself hell."

Middlecoff went out and shot a closing 71 at Pebble Beach to win the first of his two straight Crosby championships with a score of 209 for a 4-stroke margin. He holed 2 putts from thirty feet, one of them for a par on the 8th hole after his approach shot over the chasm had landed on the side of the cliff.

Byron Nelson and Ed Lowery provided a touch of yesterday by winning the pro-am with 195. Nelson's tour days were long over by 1955, but he came out of retirement on his Texas ranch to play superbly, and donated his $1,500 pro-am purse to charity. Lowery's first golfing recognition came back in 1913, when he caddied for Francis Ouimet in the U. S. Open won by Ouimet in the play-off with Harry Vardon and Ted Ray.

A headline the day before the Crosby read: "Littler Man to Beat." Gene didn't win it that year, tying for sixth, but he did . . . twenty years later.

Bing Crosby showed up briefly at the Clambake before facing surgery for kidney stones. "He's full of penicillin and various miacins," explained Maurie Luxford. "They gave him sixty-six shots." Bing replied, "I'd rather have that score on the golf course."

Cary Middlecoff and Maurie Luxford

Ed Lowery and Byron Nelson

Professional			Pro-Am	
Cary Middlecoff	69-69-71—209	$2,500	Byron Nelson—Ed Lowery	—195
Paul McGuire	68-75-70—213	1,250	Cary Middlecoff—Ed Crowley	—196
Julius Boros	70-71-72—213	1,250	Stan Leonard—Jack Walters	—197
Vic Ghezzi	69-75-71—215	600	Fred Wampler—Julie Bescos	—197
Stan Leonard	66-73-76—215	600	Bob Rosburg—Hank Mann	—197
Gene Littler	70-70-76—216	300	Julius Boros—Howard Everitt	—198
Doug Ford	67-74-75—216	300	Doug Ford—Randolph Scott	—198
Bob Rosburg	72-67-77—216	300	Gardner Dickinson—Wheeler Farish	—199
Ed Furgol	72-70-75—217	200	Art Doering—Gen. Omar Bradley	—199
Jack Burke, Jr.	69-72-76—217	200	Al Mengert—Rod Funseth	—199
Jimmy Demaret	72-71-74—217	200		

1956

THE BEST ROUND EVER?

After winning the Crosby the previous year with a 209 and a 4-stroke margin in good weather, Cary Middlecoff proved even more adept under some soggy conditions in 1956 with a 202 that won it by 5 shots.

It was the record score for a 54-hole Crosby, compiled on rounds of 66 at Cypress Point, 68 at Monterey Peninsula and a remarkable 68 in an all-day rainstorm over the final round at Pebble Beach.

The only other player in the field who shot better than 211 was Mike Souchak, who opened with a 64 at Cypress and finished at 207.

"Doc Middlecoff's 68 in that terrible weather was one of the best rounds of golf ever played, if not the best," claims Ben Hogan, who shot 81 that day. Ben, however, had delighted the gallery of 5,000 that followed him and Bing on the first round at Cypress. That day Hogan shot 67 with birdies on 14, 15 and 16.

The tournament didn't actually end until Monday morning because several foursomes were halted by darkness on Sunday. None of those players were in contention.

In the pro-am, Ralph Blomquist and George Galios had 121 after 36 holes and finished with a winning 188.

Cary Middlecoff

Ralph Blomquist and George Galios

Professional			Pro-Am	
Cary Middlecoff	66-68-68—202	$2,500	Ralph Blomquist—George Galios	—188
Mike Souchak	64-71-72—207	1,500	Don Whitt—Dr. Ed Lambert	—191
Bill Ogden	68-69-74—211	850	John Barnum—Dennis O'Keefe	—192
Bob Rosburg	69-65-77—211	850	Bud Ward—Harvie Ward	—193
Dow Finsterwald	69-69-74—212	450	Cary Middlecoff—Ed Crowley	—194
Doug Ford	70-67-75—212	450	Art Bell—Ken Venturi	—194
Bo Wininger	68-69-76—213	300	Lt. Donald Addington—Frank Pace, Jr.	—194
Mike Fetchick	65-78-71—214	200	George Buzzini—William Higgins	—195
Dutch Harrison	71-69-75—215	200	Bob Rosburg—Hank Mann	—195
Gardner Dickinson	70-70-75—215	200	Glen Spivey—Pete Geyer	—195

1957

WORTHY OF ANOTHER PURPLE HEART

Jay Hebert, who won a Purple Heart on Iwo Jima during World War II, deserved another medal for heroic golf under hostile conditions in the last Crosby to be conducted over 54 holes. Hebert shot rounds of 74-69-70 for 213 and a 2-stroke margin over Cary Middlecoff, gunning for his third straight Crosby.

Middlecoff, however, teamed with Ed Crowley to win the pro-am with a record 187, 9 shots better than Hebert and Roger Kelly.

Two native Californians left their mark in the qualifying round with 69s. They were Ken Venturi, in his professional debut, and the late Tony Lema, described in one press account as "the baby-faced-23-year-old new pro from Elko, Nevada." Lema became so excited on the 9th hole that he fell eighteen feet off a cliff, bruising his shins and elbows.

Until the tournament began, it had been the dryest California winter of the century. Bing, elated over the warm weather, went to mass one morning at Carmel . . . to hear the priest pray for rain. It fell during the second round, accompanied by high winds, and drenched the peninsula on Sunday morning. Moments after play was completed, a storm knocked out the power lines.

Jay Hebert

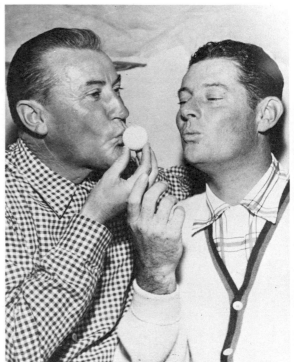

Ed Crowley and Cary Middlecoff

Professional			Pro-Am	
Jay Hebert	74-69-70—213	$2,500	Cary Middlecoff—Ed Crowley	—187
Cary Middlecoff	76-67-72—215	1,500	Jay Hebert—Roger Kelly	—196
Stan Leonard	68-74-74—216	1,000	Ed Oldfield—Ernie Nevers	—196
Walter Burkemo	72-71-76—219	700	Wesley Ellis—Boyd O'Donnell	—198
Lloyd Mangrum	73-75-72—220	350	Smiley Quick—Adolph Schmidt, Jr.	—198
Paul O'Leary	73-71-76—220	350	Gardner Dickinson—Wheeler Farish	—199
Ken Venturi	73-71-76—220	350	George Buzzini—William Higgins	—199
Wesley Ellis	76-69-75—220	350	John Zontek—Nelson Cullenward	—199
Ed Furgol	71-71-79—221	200	Al Besselink—Bob Goldwater	—199
Julius Boros	75-68-79—222	133	Bob Rosburg—Jim Wilbert	—200
Henry Williams, Jr.	71-76-75—222	133	Byron Nelson—Ed Lowery	—200
William Ogden	80-69-73—222	133	Ralph Blomquist—George Galios	—200
Harry Dee	72-72-78—222	133	Bob Gajda—Frank Tatum, Jr.	—200
Al Besselink	73-74-75—222	133	Shelley Mayfield—Bob Crosby	—200
Billy Maxwell	66-78-78—222	133		

1958

LIGHTS, CAMERA— ACTION

It was the year the Crosby went big time. The format went to 72 holes, with two rounds at Pebble Beach. The purse was elevated from $15,000 to $50,000—thanks to a $35,000 contribution from Oldsmobile—and the tournament was televised nationally for the first time.

Newlywed Kathy Crosby assisted her husband in the telecast. "She's quite a gal," mused Bing. "She even likes to cook, which is fortunate for me. She's very proficient, makes a wonderful soufflé and is adept at various salads. Has a bad stroke with the vacuum cleaner, however."

Billy Casper won with 277, breaking away from a 54-hole tie with Bob Rosburg for a closing 71, while Rosburg struggled home with an 81. Rosburg opened with a sizzling 65 at Monterey Peninsula and led by 5 strokes after 36 holes.

The runner-up with 281 was Dave Marr, making his first national impact on the tour. "He's young and hungry," observed golf historian Fred Corcoran. "We'll hear more from this fellow."

A retired Army colonel named Melvin Blair attempted to heist $100,000 from the tournament office on Sunday night, but was subdued by a deputy sheriff who feigned a heart attack while being held at gunpoint. Blair later admitted he had consumed three half-pints of whiskey before attempting the robbery.

Billy Casper

Roger Kelly and Jay Hebert

Professional			Pro-Am	
Billy Casper	71-66-69-71—277	$4,000	Jay Hebert—Roger Kelly	—260
Dave Marr	69-70-70-72—281	2,400	Billy Casper—Bob Reynolds	—261
Ken Venturi	68-74-70-72—284	1,633	Paul Harney—Phil Harris	—263
Dow Finsterwald	73-67-69-75—284	1,633	Ken Venturi—Charles French	—263
Jack Burke, Jr.	72-68-71-73—284	1,633	Johnny Pott—John Miles	—264
Jay Hebert	69-72-71-73—285	1,300	Bob Harris—Ralph Kiner	—264
Bob Harris	71-69-71-75—286	1,116	Jack Fleck—Frank Souchak	—264
Tommy Bolt	67-71-74-74—286	1,116	Dow Finsterwald—Fred Briskin	—264
Cary Middlecoff	72-69-72-73—286	1,116	Byron Nelson—Ed Lowery	—264
Bob Rosburg	65-67-74-81—287	975	Ted Kroll—Bob Goldwater	—265
Chick Harbert	71-68-74-74—287	975	Tommy Jacobs—Bob Lemon	—265

1959

WALL-TO-WALL JOB

Art Wall led Jimmy Demaret by 4 strokes and Gene Littler by 6 as he teed off the final round in 1959 at Pebble Beach. After birdies on the first three holes, Wall appeared to be a cinch.

With four holes to play, Art had a 5-shot lead. But strange things are always happening at Pebble Beach, and the situation tightened considerably when Littler took birdies on 16 and 17 as Wall bogeyed both holes.

Trailing Wall by a single stroke on the 18th tee, Littler hit his drive in play near the seawall, then hooked his second shot into the ocean. "There were so many people lined up along the water," Littler smiled ruefully, "that I thought the fairway had tilted."

Wall survived a shaky incoming 41 for a 75 and won the $4,000 first-place prize with 279. He added another $2,000 from his pro-am victory with Charlie Coe, a two-time U. S. Amateur champion.

Jimmy Demaret had a 29, with a pair of eagles, on the back nine at Monterey Peninsula. It was his first tour event since the PGA championship the previous July.

There were aces by Jim Ferree, Lloyd Mangrum and George Fazio. John Brodie also sank a tee shot on the 7th at Pebble Beach—after hitting his first shot into the water.

And Porky Oliver's record of 16 strokes on the 16th at Cypress Point was broken. Hans Merrell, a club pro from Magadore, Ohio, took 19 en route to a 94.

Charlie Coe and Art Wall

Professional			Pro-Am	
Art Wall, Jr.	69-65-70-75—279	$4,000	Art Wall, Jr.–Charlie Coe	—252
Gene Littler	73-67-70-71—281	2,150	Doug Ford—Art Anderson	—257
Jimmy Demaret	74-64-70-73—281	2,150	Gene Littler—Jack Munger	—259
John McMullin	68-73-71-71—283	1,500	Smiley Quick—Morgan Barofsky	—260
Bob Rosburg	71-70-70-72—283	1,500	Art Bell—Robert Roos, Jr.	—260
Don January	70-72-70-73—285	1,250	Jimmy Demaret—Pete Elliot	—260
Doug Ford	73-74-68-70—285	1,250	Wesley Ellis—Frank Tatum, Jr.	—262
Billy Maxwell	67-74-72-73—286	1,025	Ellsworth Vines—Willard Parker	—263
Lloyd Mangrum	73-71-70-72—286	1,025	Bob Rosburg—Nelson Cullenward	—263
Arnold Palmer	69-77-67-73—286	1,025	Gardner Dickinson—Fred Kammer, Jr.	—263
Jack Fleck	75-69-73-69—286	1,025		

1960

SAN FRANCISCO SWEEP

Crosby old-timers felt right at home in the 1960 tournament. The weather progressed from bad to awful.

An all-day rain on opening day left the golf courses squishy as quagmires for the next two rounds, and then it poured on Sunday as San Francisco's Ken Venturi splashed around for a closing 77 that gave him a 286 and first place by 3 strokes.

The tournament had a real San Francisco flavor. San Francisco city amateur champion Bob Silvestri and Bob Ward took the pro-am with a 262 to join Venturi in the winners' circle.

Gene Littler, who had crept within 2 shots of Venturi, was delayed by a ruling on the 7th hole, where he had punched his tee shot into the rocks. Littler was given a free drop, but Venturi's foursome played through and Ken was able to maintain a pace that nobody behind him could match.

"I've never been so wet in my life," brayed Johnny Weissmuller, once the world's greatest swimmer.

Venturi, with a large San Francisco delegation rooting him home, called it "the worst weather I've ever played in" and the victory the most satisfying of his career. Ken's 77 really wasn't bad. Littler had 80, Mike Souchak 82, Dow Finsterwald 83 and Lloyd Mangrum 84.

Bud Ward and Bob Silvestri

Professional

Ken Venturi	70-71-68-77—286	$4,000
Tommy Jacobs	70-74-70-75—289	2,150
Julius Boros	73-71-72-73—289	2,150
Porky Oliver	73-68-73-76—290	1,500
Don January	72-71-69-78—290	1,500
Gene Littler	67-73-71-80—291	1,250
Billy Maxwell	71-74-68-78—291	1,250
Doug Ford	73-76-70-73—292	1,100
Billy Casper	74-73-72-75—294	1,025
Paul Harney	75-73-70-76—294	1,025

Pro-Am

Bud Ward—Bob Silvestri	—262
Ken Venturi—Harvie Ward	—265
Julius Boros—Don Schwab	—265
George Bayer—Morgan Barofsky	—266
Bill Maxwell—Bob Knudson	—268
Ron Nicol—Wheeler Farish, Jr.	—269
Doug Ford—Arne Boscacci	—269
Lionel Hebert—Pete Elliot	—270
Bob Rosburg—Jim Garner	—270
Mason Rudolph—Curtis Person	—270

Ken Venturi

145

1961

ROSBURG IN A KNEE-KNOCKER

If they presented awards for the most exciting finishes in the Crosby, the 1961 tournament would be an Oscar nominee.

Bob Rosburg won it, with a closing 72 over windy Pebble Beach for 282. There were seven players within 2 strokes of that figure, and they each had a chance to win.

Roberto de Vicenzo was 20 feet past the cup on the 18th in 2. Nobody had ever seen this done before. Roberto's bid for an eagle just grazed the cup, and he was in with 283.

Dave Ragan took a double bogey on 17 to give him 283, and Bill Collins went bogey-bogey over the last two for a 284. Arnold Palmer went out in 34, came back in 41 for his 284. Dave Hill was only 4 strokes out of the lead on the first tee, but hit three balls into the ocean and shot 85.

Ted Kroll, leading Hill by 4 going into the last round, struggled around in 81.

Rosburg finished like a champion, holing a twelve-foot birdie putt on 18. "I had one coming on this golf course," he said. Rosburg had lost three times in the California Amateur finals at Pebble Beach. In the 1958 Crosby he led by 5 shots after 36 holes, shared the lead after 54 and took 81 on Sunday.

Wes Ellis and Sandy Tatum won the pro-am with 252, Tatum helping by 37 strokes.

Frank (Sandy) Tatum

Bob Rosburg

Professional

Bob Rosburg	69-67-74-72—282	$5,300
Dave Ragan	68-71-70-74—283	2,800
Roberto de Vicenzo	72-66-70-75—283	2,800
Gardner Dickinson	70-71-72-71—284	1,625
Arnold Palmer	70-68-71-75—284	1,625
Ted Kroll	69-66-68-81—284	1,625
Bill Collins	67-68-74-75—284	1,625
Johnny Pott	73-72-69-71—285	1,300
Jack Burke, Jr.	68-69-75-74—286	1,030
Bo Wininger	70-72-70-74—286	1,030
Ken Venturi	67-71-74-74—286	1,030
Dow Finsterwald	69-70-72-75—286	1,030
Marty Furgol	70-72-67-77—286	1,030

Pro-Am

Wes Ellis—Frank Tatum, Jr.	—252
Dow Finsterwald—Fred Kammer	—254
Tommy Jacobs—Wheeler Farish, Jr.	—255
Byron Nelson—Ed Lowery	—256
Ken Venturi—Harvie Ward	—259
Mason Rudolph—Curtis Person	—259
Dave Ragan—Billy Hoelle	—259
Ted Kroll—Aubrey Duffy	—259
Bob Harris—Eli Bariteau, Jr.	—260
Tom Nieporte—Gordon MacRae	—260
Jack Burke, Jr.—George Coleman	—260
Johnny Pott—James French, Jr.	—260

Wes Ellis

1962

'BUT IT NEVER SNOWS HERE'

Most people remember the 1962 Crosby because of the snow, which pushed the fourth round back to Monday. Dimmed by the passage of years were a series of clutch putts by Doug Ford that gave him the championship.

Ford holed a five-footer for a par on the 18th at Pebble Beach to tie Joe Campbell for first place at 286. Since the telecast was over, they went to the first tee for the play-off.

Campbell three-putted and Ford, after being trapped on his approach, made a six-footer to win.

Ford headed immediately for the parking lot, and was driving away when hailed by Doc Giffin, the new PGA press secretary. "It was my second week on the job," Giffin said. "I could see it going up in smoke if Doug had got away before the writers had a chance to talk with him."

Campbell had 210 after 54 holes, leading Ford by 2 shots, and he admitted during Sunday's snowy postponement that Ford was the man he feared most down the stretch.

The golfers were bundled up like skiers for the frosty final round. Campbell, wearing a woolen cap with ear muffs, held his lead until he bogeyed the 17th. Ford moved into a tie there with another clutch putt—an eight-footer for a par.

Bob McCallister and Albie Pearson won the pro-am with 255, posting an opening-round 59.

Bob McCallister

Professional

*Doug Ford	70-73-69-74—286	$5,300
Joe Campbell	67-71-72-76—286	3,400
Phil Rodgers	67-75-72-74—288	2,200
Dave Ragan	70-74-73-73—290	1,800
Ken Venturi	72-69-73-76—290	1,800
Johnny Pott	69-75-73-74—291	1,400
Mason Rudolph	68-77-71-75—291	1,400
Tommy Jacobs	71-75-70-75—291	1,400
Don Massengale	72-76-73-71—292	1,000
Paul Harney	70-76-73-73—292	1,000
Butch Baird	74-73-73-72—292	1,000
Bernard Hunt	70-76-70-76—292	1,000
Stan Leonard	74-74-71-73—292	1,000
Ted Kroll	74-75-68-75—292	1,000

* Won play-off

Pro-Am

Bob McCallister–Albie Pearson	—255
Stan Leonard–Bud Taylor	—261
Dow Finsterwald–Fred Kammer, Jr.	—261
Doug Ford–Dudley Wysong	—262
Doug Sanders–Lloyd Fitzer	—265
Tommy Jacobs–Wheeler Farish, Jr.	—266
Billy Maxwell–Bob Knudson	—266
Al Mengert–Bob Goldwater	—266
George Bayer–Morgan Barofsky	—268
Miller Barber–O'Hara Watts	—268

Doug Ford

1963

PUTT-PUTT-PUTT

Billy Casper sweated out his second Crosby championship in front of a television set in the press room at Del Monte Lodge, watching nervously as Gary Player, Bob Duden and Jack Nicklaus squandered their opportunities down the stretch.

Casper had finished early with 74 for 285. Player took a bogey on 17 and then missed a twelve-foot birdie putt on 18 to post 286. Duden, putting with a pendulum style, rolled his birdie attempt for a tie four feet past, and missed the short one to fall 2 strokes back.

Nicklaus looked like a cinch for at least a tie after he hooked his approach onto the green around a tree, but Jack knocked his first putt five feet past and then missed *his* second one to finish at 286.

The weather was perfect, a blessing ascribed to the fact that two priests, Father John Durkin and Father Len Scannell, were in the field for the first time. "They are going to be regular entrants," promised Bing, "from now on."

Wrote Prescott Sullivan in the San Francisco *Examiner*:

Largely dependent on hurricanes, blizzards and other meteorological disturbances for something to write about when covering the Crosby, scores of sports columnists were left without visible means of support when these sources failed them.

The pro-am champs were Doug Sanders and Lloyd Pitzer with a 257.

Billy Casper

Doug Sanders

Professional			Pro-Am	
Billy Casper	73-65-73-74—285	$5,300	Doug Sanders—Lloyd Pitzer	—257
Bob Rosburg	71-74-70-71—286	2,140	Bob Duden—Ted Gleichmann	—260
Dave Hill	68-69-76-73—286	2,140	Tommy Jacobs—Wheeler Farish, Jr.	—260
Art Wall, Jr.	71-71-72-72—286	2,140	Jay Hebert—Roger Kelly	—261
Gary Player	73-69-70-74—286	2,140	George Bayer—Morgan Barofsky	—261
Jack Nicklaus	71-69-76-70—286	2,140	Julius Boros—Don Schwab	—262
Bob Duden	70-73-67-77—287	1,400	Dave Hill—Phil Harris	—263
Julius Boros	66-75-70-77—288	1,200	Mason Rudolph—Curtis Person	—263
George Bayer	68-73-71-76—288	1,200	Bob Rosburg—John Brodie	—264
Doug Sanders	74-74-69-71—288	1,200	Jack Burke, Jr.—George Coleman	—264
			Rex Baxter—Mike Riley	—264

1964

ALTAR BOY POPS THE CORK

Tony Lema served mass at Carmel Mission on the final morning of the tournament and served champagne to the press that night.

It was an intriguing sequence for the colorful pro from San Leandro, California, who died in an air crash two and a half years later after carving a brilliant, if brief, record on the tour.

Tony won the 1964 Crosby by 3 strokes with 284, shooting 76 in the final round at Pebble Beach on a stormy day. He also teamed with Father John Durkin to finish second in the pro-am, 1 stroke behind the winning score of 259 by Mike Fetchick and Charles Seaver.

"We would have won," remarked Father Durkin, "but I only had a gallon of holy water left."

Lema credited the presence of the priest as a tremendous benefit to him mentally, physically and spiritually. "He had a calming influence on me when things looked bleak," Tony said. "I couldn't swear."

Tony was an altar boy for Father Durkin in the Sunday morning service and then served mass for him. As the rain poured and the winds raged in the afternoon, Lema methodically avoided serious pitfalls at Pebble Beach to give the Bay Area its third Crosby champion, following the triumphs of Ken Venturi in 1960 and Bob Rosburg in 1961.

Charlie Seaver

Tony Lema

Professional

Tony Lema	70-68-70-76—284	$5,800
Gay Brewer	76-68-70-73—287	3,100
Bo Wininger	69-73-70-75—287	3,100
Al Geiberger	80-67-68-73—288	2,150
Tommy Aaron	70-68-73-77—288	2,150
George Knudson	72-76-68-73—289	1,650
Gardner Dickinson	71-73-70-75—289	1,650
Bruce Devlin	69-67-74-79—289	1,650
Dave Marr	72-69-72-76—289	1,650
Bob Charles	68-71-76-75—290	1,250
Dow Finsterwald	70-73-69-78—290	1,250
Billy Casper	71-68-75-76—290	1,250
Paul Harney	76-71-66-77—290	1,250

Pro-Am

Mike Fetchick—Charles Seaver	—258
Tony Lema—Father John Durkin	—259
Rex Baxter—Bud Taylor	—261
Phil Rodgers—Jim Vickers	—262
George Bayer—Morgan Barofsky	—262
Dave Ragan—Billy Hoelle	—262
Don January—Potts Berglund	—264
Ken Venturi—Roane Puett	—264
Peter Butler—O'Hara Watts	—265
Richard Crawford—Wade Walker	—265
Art Wall, Jr.—Alvin Dark	—265
George Knudson—Jim Backus	—265
Gay Brewer—Jim Hill	—265
Al Geiberger—Ted Gleichman	—265
Ernie Vossler—Bill Higgins	—265
Arnold Palmer—Mark McCormack	—265
Gardner Dickinson—Dick Davies	—265
Jerry Steelsmith—H. Rodriguez	—265
Chi Chi Rodriguez—Bob Cardinal	—265

1965

IT OUGHT TO BE A LESSON

Late in the afternoon the day before the tournament opened, Bruce Crampton took a forty-five-minute lesson in alignment from Jack Nicklaus. The results weren't apparent in the first round, Crampton shooting 75, but the laconic Australian pulled his game together over the last 54 holes to compile a 284 and beat Tony Lema, the defending champion, by 3 strokes.

Crampton won it by chipping in from 55 feet for a birdie on 15 the final day, moments before Lema missed a short birdie putt.

The pro-am championship was shared at 260 by the teams of George Bayer-Morgan Barofsky and George Archer-Nelson Cullenward.

The weather was favorable early in the week, but by Saturday it turned grim enough, in the words of the late Alfred Wright of *Sports Illustrated*, "to send the witches of Macbeth fleeing their caldrons and flying for cover."

Ben Hogan was on hand as a spectator, looking over some new prospects for his company. It was also the year of the Honeymoon Express, a cross-country odyssey in a golf car by newlyweds John and Jean Drawz of Minnesota in a 3M promotion that culminated at Pebble Beach.

Bruce Crampton

Nelson Cullenward

Professional				Pro-Am	
Bruce Crampton	75-67-73-69—284	$7,500		George Bayer—Morgan Barofsky	—260
Tony Lema	71-65-79-72—287	4,000		George Archer—Nelson Cullenward	—260
Jack Nicklaus	72-68-77-71—288	3,100		Gene Littler—Lou Oehmig	—262
Billy Casper	70-70-76-72—288	3,100		Johnny Pott—Jimmy Day	—263
Al Mengert	78-67-74-70—289	2,450		Charles Coody—Bob Cardinal	—263
Harold Kneece	69-76-69-75—289	2,450		Lionel Hebert—Roger Kelly	—263
Ken Still	76-69-75-70—290	1,833		Sam Carmichael—Alvin Dark	—263
Jack Cupit	77-69-69-75—290	1,833		Dan Sikes—Johnny Thornton	—264
Rocky Thompson	74-70-68-78—290	1,833		Al Mengert—Jim Davenport	—265
Terry Wilcox	72-74-71-74—291	1,400		Julius Boros—Don Schwab	—265
Jon Gustin	70-72-76-73—291	1,400		Harold Kneece—Bobby Knowles	—265
Mike Fetchick	74-69-78-70—291	1,400		Tal Smith—Jackie Jensen	—265
				Jerry Pittman—Howard Keel	—265

1966

TARDY ANNIVERSARY

They billed it as the 25th anniversary of the tournament, but it was time for the Crosby to admit publicly that it was really the 26th. When the tournament was moved to Pebble Beach in 1947, Larry Crosby was asked how many had been held at Rancho Santa Fe. "Five," replied Larry, but a recheck later disclosed it to be six.

"You really couldn't count that first one in 1937 anyway," Larry said. "It was more of a duck hunt than a golf tournament."

So the posters proclaimed 1966 as the silver anniversary, with the appropriate explanation. The error was perpetuated rather than confuse anyone who had saved the programs, as many had. Ray Bolger joined Bing to host a television special called "The Road to Pebble Beach."

It turned out to be one of the most exciting Crosbys ever, played in favorable weather. Don Massengale, starting the final round 4 strokes behind leader Al Geiberger, holed a 45-foot eagle putt on the second hole and made a crucial five-foot birdie putt on the 18th to win his first tour event with 283.

The runner-up, a stroke back, was Arnold Palmer despite a heroic finish in which he birdied three of the last four holes.

In the pro-am, Billy Martindale and Bob Roos blew a 7-stroke lead over the final round, tied for first and lost in a sudden-death play-off to Chuck Courtney and Dr. John Moler.

Don Massengale

Chuck Courtney

Professional

Don Massengale	70-67-76-70—283	$11,000
Arnold Palmer	70-70-73-71—284	6,200
Bill Martindale	72-71-69-73—285	4,000
Al Geiberger	68-74-67-76—285	4,000
Doug Sanders	75-70-71-71—287	3,050
Randy Glover	73-72-72-70—287	3,050
R. H. Sikes	74-74-70-71—289	2,366
Jack Rule	75-70-70-74—289	2,366
Joe Campbell	71-75-73-70—289	2,366
Mason Rudolph	74-74-70-72—290	1,950
Bob Goalby	74-74-67-75—290	1,950

Pro-Am

Chuck Courtney—John Moler	—255
Bill Martindale—Bob Roos, Jr.	—255
Arnold Palmer—Mark McCormack	—256
Randy Glover—Don Schwab	—257
Gay Brewer—Dale Morey	—258
Mike Souchak—Frank Souchak	—259
Dean Refram—Richard Crane	—260
Jimmy Powell—Bill Swederskas	—260
Don Bies—William Rudkin	—260
Joe Carr—Jim Mahoney	—261
Jack Fleck—Bob Knudson	—261
Bob Goalby—Julie Bescos	—261

1967

THE RETURN OF LONG JOHN SILVER

There were three major issues in the 1967 Crosby—the debut of Spyglass Hill as a tournament site, the return of some old-fashioned Crosby weather and the emergence of Jack Nicklaus as a first-time champion.

Spyglass, the Robert Trent Jones creation in the Del Monte Forest, replaced the Dunes Course of the Monterey Peninsula Country Club as one of the three tournament sites. The pros greeted the new course warily, concerned over its length and the condition of its greens, but in the end they should have worried more about the awesome skills of Nicklaus.

In his sixth appearance at the Crosby, Jack destroyed the field with a 284 that beat Billy Casper by 5 strokes and Arnold Palmer by 7.

Mike and Frank Souchak used their big-muscle game for a victory in the pro-am with 259.

After forty-one straight days of favorable weather, the peninsula was struck by a Saturday storm that washed out play at 1:07 P.M. "The sand is blowing into the eyes of the players on seven and eight at Pebble Beach," explained PGA tournament director Jack Tuthill, "and the falling limbs on Cypress and Spyglass are endangering lives."

The tournament resumed on Sunday, despite sodden fairways, and ended on Monday.

Mike and Frank Souchak, Jack Nicklaus

Professional			Pro-Am	
Jack Nicklaus	69-73-74-68—284	$16,000	Mike Souchak—Frank Souchak	—259
Billy Casper	72-74-69-74—289	9,600	Chuck Courtney—John Moler	—262
Arnold Palmer	74-75-67-75—291	6,000	Ted Makalena—Paul Spengler	—262
Bob Rosburg	72-75-72-74—293	3,493	Al Geiberger—Lew Leis	—262
Jack Burke, Jr.	70-75-74-74—293	3,493	Wes Ellis—Frank Tatum, Jr.	—264
Bill Parker	75-72-70-76—293	3,493	Jack Burke, Jr.—Virgil Sherrill	—264
Doug Sanders	73-78-72-71—294	2,040	Tom Nieporte—Richard Remsen	—265
Dave Hill	73-80-70-71—294	2,040	Bill Collins—James Fisher	—265
Frank Beard	72-75-75-72—294	2,040	Ernie Vossler—Bill Higgins	—266
Gardner Dickinson	75-74-73-72—294	2,040	Doug Sanders—Ed Crowley	—266
Howie Johnson	73-76-72-73—294	2,040	Bob Rosburg—John Brodie	—266
Bob McCallister	73-71-75-75—294	2,040		
Wes Ellis	73-75-71-75—294	2,040		
Al Geiberger	70-77-71-76—294	2,040		

1968

POTT BY A CHIP

Jack Nicklaus was on hand to defend his Crosby championship, and Bing picked him to win again, but the champion turned out to be Johnny Pott in one of the most improbable finishes in the tournament's history.

Pott chipped in from 26 feet on the first play-off hole to beat Billy Casper and Bruce Devlin, in the first sudden-death windup at Pebble Beach since 1962. That earned him $16,000 and he picked up another $2,700 by winning the pro-am with former Navy flier Virgil Sherrill at 253.

The weather was gorgeous, for a change. Over 25,000 spectators turned out for Saturday's round, a Crosby record, but the crowd fell off Sunday, presumably because so many Bay Area fans were watching the telecast of Oakland's losing effort against Green Bay in the Super Bowl.

Bing had to write fifty-five amateurs and tell them they were being replaced by new blood. Among the newcomers was a man who wrote Bing, after watching Robert Goulet hack his way up the 18th fairway the year before, "I can play better than that guy."

Phil Harris had a painful tooth extraction on Friday afternoon, and required some extra medication bottled in Tennessee, but he was on hand for the dedication of the 3M-sponsored Bing Crosby Hall of Fame plaque at the Del Monte Lodge.

Johnny Pott

Professional			Pro-Am	
*Johnny Pott	70-71-71-73—285	$16,000	Johnny Pott—Virgil Sherrill	—253
Billy Casper	73-69-73-70—285	7,800	Billy Casper—Bob Dickson	—257
Bruce Devlin	73-69-73-70—285	7,800	Ron Cerrudo—Harvey Ward	—258
Deane Beman	74-71-72-70—287	4,000	Marty Fleckman—John Cain	—259
Ray Floyd	79-68-71-70—288	3,066	Wes Ellis—Frank Tatum, Jr.	—259
George Knudson	73-71-74-70—288	3,066	Jack Nicklaus—Bob Hoag	—259
Bobby Nichols	76-68-72-72—288	3,066	Paul Bondeson—Tom Culligan	—260
Jack Nicklaus	71-75-70-73—289	2,480	Frank Beard—Mickey Van Gerbig	—261
Jack Rule	73-76-69-72—290	2,240	Tom Nieporte—Richard Remsen	—261
Dale Douglass	75-73-73-70—291	1,840	Chick Evans—Bob Falkenburg	—261
Miller Barber	74-75-71-71—291	1,840		
Dave Hill	69-77-73-72—291	1,840		
Tony Jacklin	72-75-71-73—291	1,840		
* Won play-off				

153

1969

THE CADDIE CHAMPION

George Archer's first income at Pebble Beach was $50 as caddie for Art Bell in the 1957 Crosby. Twelve years later Archer walked out of the Del Monte Lodge with a check for $25,000, his reward for first place.

Archer was running a ranch in 1969 at nearby Gilroy, California, and he employed his local knowledge of the course for a steady performance in some of the worst weather in Crosby history.

The first round was washed out, and there was heavy doubt that the tournament could be played at all. Rains that had fallen for ten straight days turned the peninsula courses into quagmires.

It was too much for Arnold Palmer, who suggested—seriously—that the Crosby be shifted to autumn dates. "They keep calling this bad weather unusual," Palmer said, "but almost every time I've played here it rains. That's unusual?"

Bob Dickson, Dale Douglass and Howie Johnson shared second place at 284, Douglass leading with 210 after 54 holes. Dickson grabbed top money in the pro-am, teaming up with actor Jack Ging for a slick 257.

Art Bell, incidentally, missed his first Crosby in twenty-eight years. The Pebble Beach pro admitted the weather was simply too hazardous for his fifty-nine-year-old bones.

George Archer

Professional			Pro-Am	
George Archer	72-68-72-71—283	$25,000	Bob Dickson—Jack Ging	—257
Bob Dickson	73-69-74-68—284	9,666	Billy Casper—Mike Bonnallack	—258
Dale Douglass	71-69-70-74—284	9,666	Gene Littler—Dr. John Moler	—258
Howie Johnson	71-69-71-73—284	9,666	Tom Nieporte—Richard Remsen	—258
John Lotz	71-75-67-72—285	5,125	Tom Shaw—Richard Crane	—258
Jack Nicklaus	71-73-73-70—287	4,500	Jack Nicklaus—Bob Hoag	—259
Lee Elder	71-75-73-70—288	4,000	Frank Beard—Mickey Van Gerbig	—259
Bill Collins	71-73-76-69—289	2,901	Al Geiberger—Lew Leis	—259
Bruce Devlin	69-75-78-67—289	2,901	Dale Douglass—Charles de Bretteville	—260
Rod Funseth	72-71-73-73—289	2,901	Lionel Hebert—Roger Kelly	—260
Gene Littler	73-74-70-72—289	2,901	Bob McCallister—Gray Madison	—260
Don Massengale	72-75-70-72—289	2,901		
Jim Howell	73-76-68-72—289	2,901		

1970

CHARM OF THE VOODOO

Two weeks before the tournament, an amateur meteorologist from Berkeley named John Grove predicted perfect weather for the Crosby. "I've studied every single day's rainfall for the San Francisco area since 1849," Grove explained. "It goes in orderly cycles. The Crosby conditions will be excellent."

Grove was right on. The weather was beautiful throughout the tournament, and nobody enjoyed it more than Bert Yancey, who shot 278 to beat Jack Nicklaus by a stroke.

Yancey credited a $7.50 copper bracelet, a "Voodoo Bracelet" as he called it. Bert got it to correct an arthritic condition in his elbow. "It kept my mind off Nicklaus," Yancey said later.

Billy Casper was disqualified on the morning of the final round when his caddie, Del Taylor, failed to show for the 7 A.M. tee-off. The caddie had Casper's clubs. "It wasn't his fault," said Casper. "They told him I was teeing off at eight."

The pro-am winners were a couple of Stanford grads, Bob Rosburg and John Brodie, with 252.

As a concession to the NBC cameras, play began at the 10th tee at Pebble Beach the final round and wound up on the 9th green. The 10th tee is tucked away in a far corner of the course and the players had to be transported by bus.

Bert Yancey

John Brodie

Professional

Bert Yancey	67-70-72-69—278	$25,000
Jack Nicklaus	70-72-72-65—279	14,300
Bobby Nichols	71-73-69-70—283	7,350
Howie Johnson	68-74-71-70—283	7,350
John Jacobs	74-72-69-69—284	4,327
Don Massengale	70-70-70-74—284	4,327
Paul Harney	69-72-72-71—284	4,327
George Archer	68-73-71-72—284	4,327
Tom Weiskopf	71-76-68-70—285	3,000
Bob Stone	72-74-68-71—285	3,000
Rod Funseth	74-68-68-75—285	3,000
Bob Goalby	67-72-71-75—285	3,000

Pro-Am

Bob Rosburg—John Brodie	—252
Mason Rudolph—Morgan Barofsky	—253
Richard Martinez—Tom Thompson	—255
Mac Hunter—Jack Bariteau	—255
Bob Dickson—Jack Ging	—255
Dick Lotz—John Huiskamp	—255
Roberta Bernardini—Howard Keel	—256
Jack Nicklaus—Robert Hoag	—256
John Miller—Charles de Limur	—256
Ramon Sota—Jose Gancedo	—257

1971

BLONDS DO HAVE MORE FUN

Midway through the final round of the 1971 Crosby the thermometer on Stillwater Cove, just off the 7th green at Pebble Beach, read 78 degrees. About that time Arnold Palmer was getting rather warm himself, with an eagle 3 on the second hole and a birdie on the fourth to move into the lead.

The weather cooled off later in the day, however, and so did Palmer, enabling bubbly Tom Shaw to breeze home with a score of 278 to beat Arnold by 2 strokes.

Shaw gave it the casual approach, chatting with the marshals and the gallery. He led Palmer by 4 shots at one point on the back nine, and the spectators fled Pebble Beach to catch the Super Bowl on their television sets.

Lou Graham and Father John Durkin wrapped up the pro-am with 254, the priest helping Graham by 29 shots despite a hooking problem. After watching the padre slash his tee shot into the crowd on 16, Phil Harris remarked, "Father, you've already bagged your limit for the day."

It was the thirtieth and final Crosby for Maurie Luxford, who died later in the winter of a heart attack.

Rainfall early in the week made the fairways soggy, but PGA officials ruled the contestants had to play the ball as it lie. "They ought to have their heads examined for that ruling," snapped Jack Nicklaus, in a rare display of anger.

Father John Durkin and Lou Graham

Professional

Tom Shaw	68-71-69-70—278	$27,000
Arnold Palmer	72-68-69-71—280	15,400
Bob Murphy	71-69-73-69—282	9,570
Jerry Heard	72-74-71-67—284	5,581
Tom Weiskopf	71-73-68-72—284	5,581
Howie Johnson	69-70-71-74—284	5,581
Bobby Nichols	68-72-71-74—285	4,320
John Miller	73-74-72-67—286	3,666
Miller Barber	74-69-71-72—286	3,666
Dave Eichelberger	72-71-72-72—286	3,666

Pro-Am

Lou Graham—Father John Durkin	—254
Jack Burke, Jr.—George Coleman	—255
Tony Clecak—Grant Fitts	—257
Jerry Heard—Downey Orrick	—258
Tom Shaw—Ed Crowley	—260
Larry Ziegler—Max Baer	—260
Gary Loustalot—Alvin Dark	—261
Doug Ford—Ian McNab	—261
Jimmy Wright—Guy de la Valdene	—261
Larry Hinson—Andy Williams	—261

Tom Shaw

WARMING
UP FOR
THE OPEN

All sorts of interesting things happened at the 1972 Crosby. It was the first year that a pro's money winnings were officially counted in the PGA exemption listings and the first time that amateurs had to play with their regular handicaps instead of getting the customary bump of a few strokes. The weather was so balmy that the greens had to be watered for the first time in the tournament's history.

Among the amateur entries was Governor Wendell Anderson of Minnesota, a Democrat who commemorated the election year by observing that Pebble Beach must have been designed by a Republican. Also on hand was Admiral Alan Shepard with the 6-iron he used for his moon shot on the Apollo 14 space mission.

The Crosby served as a prelude to the U. S. Open, held later that year at Pebble Beach, and the winner in both was Jack Nicklaus.

Nicklaus shared the 72-hole Crosby lead with Johnny Miller at 284, Miller forfeiting his chance for outright victory with a classic shank of a 7-iron approach on 16. The play-off began on the 15th hole, and Nicklaus ended it right there with a birdie putt from twenty-five feet.

Lee Trevino and Don Schwab ran away with the pro-am by 4 strokes with 256. Trevino admitted he couldn't keep his eyes off the decorative gallery. "I ain't seen so many pretty girls," he purred, "since leaving El Paso."

Don Schwab and Lee Trevino

Jack Nicklaus

Professional

*Jack Nicklaus	66-74-71-73—284	$28,000
John Miller	75-68-67-74—284	16,000
Lee Trevino	69-74-70-73—286	9,900
Fred Marti	72-73-71-71—287	6,160
Bruce Crampton	73-72-69-73—287	6,160
Bob Murphy	76-74-69-69—288	4,357
George Archer	76-73-69-70—288	4,357
Dan Sikes	76-72-66-74—288	4,357
Tony Jacklin	70-70-71-77—288	4,357
Kermit Zarley	72-73-74-70—289	3,080
Tom Weiskopf	70-73-75-71—289	3,080
Mac Hunter	76-73-68-72—289	3,080
Gay Brewer	75-72-68-74—289	3,080

* Won play-off.

Pro-Am

Lee Trevino–Don Schwab	—256
Bob Murphy–Tommy Vickers	—260
Dale Douglass–John Archer	—261
Sam Snead–Ed Tutwiler	—265
Dave Stockton–Bud Bradley	—265
George Archer–Robert Roos	—265
Don Bies–William Rudkin	—265
Tom Weiskopf–John Swanson	—265
Bobby Nichols–Glen Campbell	—266
Orville Moody–Dan Moss	—267
Hale Irwin–Darius Keaton	—267

1973

ORVILLE'S COSTLY YIP

All Orville Moody had to do to win a $36,000 check and his first tournament since 1969 was get down in two putts from 25 feet on the 18th green of Pebble Beach. He lagged to within 2½ feet, but he missed from there, and went to No. 15 for a play-off with Jack Nicklaus and Raymond Floyd.

That was all for Orville Moody in the 1973 Crosby, because Nicklaus rolled in a twelve-foot birdie putt on the first play-off hole and Moody had to settle instead for the consolation check of $16,650.

"I felt sorry for Orville," Jack was to say later. "He hasn't won in a long time, but a tournament is 72 holes and you've got to putt the last green, too."

It was all the more painful for Moody, since he had taken a 4-stroke lead into the final round. He threw it away with a 76, and he approached the prospect of facing Nicklaus in the play-off with all the hope of a man at the guillotine.

The long day kept the ABC television cameras grinding more than an hour over the allotted time, and the play-off ended just as darkness descended over the peninsula. "If it had gone another hole," admitted Bing, "I don't know what we would have done."

Lanny Wadkins and Billy Satterfield won the pro-am with a 255, Satterfield helping his pro on 37 strokes.

Jack Nicklaus

Lanny Wadkins

Professional			Pro-Am	
*Jack Nicklaus	71-69-71-71—282	$36,000	Lanny Wadkins—Billy Satterfield	—255
Orville Moody	71-66-69-76—282	16,650	Jim Simons—Garth Reynolds	—262
Ray Floyd	71-70-70-71—282	16,650	Billy Casper—Howard Kaskel	—264
Dave Marr	71-71-70-73—285	8,460	Dave Stockton—Bud Bradley	—265
Rod Funseth	72-74-71-69—286	6,930	Terry Wilcox—Bill Celli	—266
Lee Elder	76-68-69-73—286	6,930	Jack Lewis—Mauricio Urdaneta	—267
Billy Casper	66-67-78-76—287	5,535	Mac McLendon—David Kirkland	—268
Don Iverson	72-68-70-77—287	5,535	Orville Moody—Bill Flowers	—269
Butch Baird	72-72-75-69—288	4,320	Tom Weiskopf—Jim Mahoney	—269
Lee Trevino	74-70-73-71—288	4,320	Al Geiberger—Lew Leis	—269
Howie Johnson	73-71-73-71—288	4,320	Tommy Jacobs—Alvin Dark	—269
Gibby Gilbert	74-67-73-74—288	4,320	Mason Rudolph—Morgan Barofsky	—269
* Won play-off				

1974

Did Eldon Dedini know something? The cover drawn by the famous artist for the 1974 Crosby tournament program depicted a golfer, pants rolled above the knees, standing in deep water and smiling in surprise as a mermaid rises out of the waves to present him with a golf ball.

The weather turned out to be far more suitable for mermaids than golf as heavy rain fell continually throughout the week and finally ended the competition at 54 holes. It was, in the words of television announcer Chris Schenkel, "a very depressing tournament," compounded by the absence of Bing, hospitalized with a lung infection which later required surgery.

Tournament dates were traded with the Los Angeles Open, and the Crosby opened the tour on January 3, requiring the qualifying round to be played December 31. The galleries were thinned further by the gasoline shortage.

Thursday's round was washed out, and hail stopped play for nearly two hours on Saturday. The fourth round, scheduled for Monday, could not get under way. Finally at 4 P.M. the tournament was called after 54 holes.

The winner was Johnny Miller with a score of 208, splendid golf under the prevailing conditions. Miller also won the pro-am with Locke de Bretteville, with a 196. "It's just as well they called it," Miller joked afterward. "Locke was starting to choke."

Johnny Miller

Locke de Bretteville

Professional			Pro-Am	
Johnny Miller	68-70-70—208	$27,750	Johnny Miller–Locke de Bretteville	—196
Grier Jones	71-69-72—212	15,817	B. R. McLendon–David Kirkland	—197
Bruce Summerhays	74-71-69—214	6,764	Hubert Green–Louis Auer	—198
Rod Funseth	72-70-72—214	6,764	Dwaine Knight–James Murray III	—198
John Jacobs	74-68-72—214,	6,764	Billy Casper–Howard Kaskel	—198
Tom Kite	71-75-68—214	6,764	Don Bies–William Rudkin	—198
David Glenz	70-72-73—215	4,266	Steve Melnyk–Ogden Phipps	—199
Dave Eichelberger	69-74-72—215	4,266	Hale Irwin–Darius Keaton	—200
Bob Eastwood	71-71-74—216	3,075	Lanny Wadkins–Billy Satterfield	—200
Bob E. Smith	74-75-67—216	3,075	Herb Hooper–Hank Ketcham	—201
Bruce Crampton	73-72-71—216	3,075	Bobby Nichols–Glen Campbell	—201
Dave Stockton	73-70-73—216	3,075	Jim Wiechers–Vern Peak	—201
Mike Morley	76-69-71—216	3,075	Maurice Ver Brugge–Morse Erskine	—201
Barney Thompson	67-75-74—216	3,075	Mike Morley–Jamie Gough III	—201

1975

GENE WINS THE JACK-JOHNNY SHOW

The 1975 Crosby had all the ingredients of a promoter's dream. Here was native Californian Johnny Miller, fresh from his record-shattering victories at Phoenix and Tucson—a two-week odyssey in which he was 49 strokes under par. And here was the man he feared most, Jack Nicklaus, coming out of a winter hibernation in Florida to challenge him.

Miller and Nicklaus were the cynosures of all eyes early in the week, interviewed incessantly about each other. The confrontation drew the largest Crosby press ever, including a foreign delegation eager for the showdown.

It never happened. Neither Jack nor Johnny could get going, and when it was over the champion was forty-four-year-old Gene Littler, a victim of cancer surgery less than three years earlier.

Except for fog late in the day Saturday and the wind on Sunday, the weather was good. Bing was back in the TV booth, fully recovered, and the tournament set an all-time gate receipt record of nearly $600,000.

The pro-am winners were Bruce Devlin and Jacky Lee, the former pro quarterback, with 260.

Gene Littler

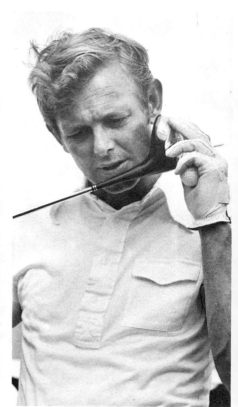

Bruce Devlin

Professional				Pro-Am	
Gene Littler	68-71-68-73—280	$37,000		Bruce Devlin—Jacky Lee	—260
Hubert Green	66-75-74-69—284	21,090		Tom Watson—Robert Willits	—263
Tom Kite	70-76-69-70—285	13,135		Hubert Green—Louis Auer	—263
Lou Graham	72-70-70-75—287	8,695		Bruce Crampton—Joe Denton	—267
Forrest Fezler	71-73-72-72—288	7,585		Rod Curl—Tom Culligan	—268
Jack Nicklaus	71-74-72-72—289	5,318		Allen Miller—Dan Searle, Jr.	—269
Dave Hill	76-72-69-72—289	5,318		Gene Littler—John Moler	—269
Rik Massengale	72-71-74-72—289	5,318		Jim Simons—Garth Reynolds	—269
Len Thompson	74-71-71-73—289	5,318		Lou Graham—Father John Durkin	—269
Johnny Miller	71-74-70-74—289	5,318		Joe Inman—Mauricio Urdaneta	—270
Bruce Devlin	73-71-69-76—289	5,318		B. R. McLendon—George Burns III	—270